CANDLE MAGIK
MAGIK FOR EVERYONE

DAVID THOMPSON

CANDLE MAGIK

MAGIK FOR EVERYONE

DAVID THOMPSON

ISBN: 978-1-961765-08-5

Front Cover photo ID 276270406 © Vera Petruk | Dreamstime.com

Back cover by: David Thompson

To Fortuna, Goddess of Fortune

"They say rather than cursing the darkness, one should light a candle. They don't mention anything about cursing a lack of candles." — George Carlin

CHAPTER ONE

Manifestation or Magik?

Two different words, both mean the same thing: Imposing our will onto the surrounding reality. Making things happen. Tilting the playing field in our favor. Nudging the dice of fate to favor us, not the other people. It often doesn't take much. A slight wiggle, a minute's delay in starting a trip, can place you onto the path of a new lifestyle, a new life partner, finding that perfect car or house,

For example, a space agency sent a probe to an asteroid. They nudged it. The results are that the asteroid shifted slightly in its orbit.

And this is also what magik does. It sends out tendrils of energy to nudge the course of reality coming at you, to set you on a somewhat different course.

What magik cannot do: Force another to take actions that is against their nature or will. Magik can't drastically modify your life's course swiftly. Magik can't make your perfect soul-mate appear on your doorstep. If you desire huge changes, be prepared for a series of rituals, all working towards the same goal.

Much like a spaceship in space, it takes more energy to shift the orbit around a planet. Tiny shifts over a long period will do the trick. And, like that spaceship, certain areas of the orbit change simpler and easier.

Candle magik involves the use of candles in ritual. It is a form of sympathetic magik, wherein the candle is lit and its flame is used to transmit the desired intention. The color of the candle, its size, the type of oil used, and the words spoken during the ritual all contribute to the strength of the spell.

Candle magik can be used for protection, banishing, healing, and to manifest one's desired outcome. It can also send energy to a specific person or situation. The ritual is often accompanied by visualizations, affirmations, and vocalization of the desired outcome. The power of the ritual is often enhanced by the use of crystals, herbs, and other natural objects.

Why "Magik" and not "Magic"?

If you are new to magik, you might wonder why it's sometimes spelled "magick" or "magik".

This started early in the 20th century, when Aleister Crowley started using the word "magick" and gave several reasons. The most often mentioned reason is to differentiate what he was doing from stage magic. I tend to drop the "c", as do many other writers.

It's just a word.

Just like many consider the topic of magik to be occult.

Occult is another term for "hidden". In the past, people who indulged themselves in magik would sometimes find them pulling away from others. In my case, I wound up with a house-mate who vehemently rejected any magik. This opposition is fear-based, with little evidence to back-up their fear.

And, in contrast to many people, those who vehemently oppose something have little room left in their minds to alter their viewpoint.

So, sometimes it's best to stay hidden. Even if you are working magik out in the open, using simple candles.

What makes this book different?

I tend to inject some odd humor into my writing. Plus, my own personal experiences with candle magik will also contribute to this book in many, many ways.

It all started when I was in this small and unique new Age bookshop in South Austin. I happened to find a book on candle magik.

Oh, not just ANY book, but a book that simplified the entire process into a very easy set of rituals to use candles by themselves for magik. It was from a small press, and it is long, long out of print. This book was unfortunately lost, either lost during a move or loaned to a friend, and never returned.

In fact, many searches have yet to even locate an archived

listing for this book. Doesn't help that I have forgotten the title, much less the author.

One unusual aspect of this book was the inclusion of a lunar ephemeris in the appendix, which assisted me in timing my rituals. This was because the entire concept behind such magik depends on the phase of the moon.

It was pretty simple, really. One divides the month into two phases, based upon the moon's phase. The BRING phase. Then the RELEASE phase.

The BRING phase begins the day of, or night of, the New Moon. This lasts until 2 days before the Full Moon. The RELEASE phase begins the day/night after the Full Moon until 1 day prior to the New Moon.

Like that book, in the back of this book will be a chart of New and Full moon times in United States Eastern Time and Universal Coordinated Time (UTC, GMT - Greenwich Mean Time), which you will need to adjust for your time zone.

For example, the Bring Cycle might begin on a Tuesday at 18:00 UTC (6:00 p.m.). Let's say you live in Austin, Texas, which is in United States Central Standard Time. To convert 18:00 UTC (6:00 p.m.) into your local time, subtract 6 hours to get 12 noon CST. During daylight saving (summer) time, you would only subtract 5 hours, so 18:00 UTC would convert to 1:00 p.m CDT. Note that the U.S. uses a 12-hour format with a.m. and p.m.

Don't worry, I have provided a link to a time zone website. Just input the UTC time and date, and then your location. It'll handle the rest. I did not have this type of utility handy when I first started, so there was a lot of head scratching, especially after the daylight savings shift.

The History and Origins of Candle magik

None of my books would be complete without a brief history on the subject - and this book is no different.

The practice of candle magik has been a part of human history for thousands of years and is both rich and fascinating. When deep diving into the history of candles, it becomes clear that candles magik has a rich and fascinating past, dating back to some of the most ancient civilizations, such as Egypt, Greece, and Rome, where candles were revered as a potent medium for connecting with the divine and channeling their energy. Of course, candles were also used for light, as well as oil lamps. Until the harnessing of electricity and the invention of the light-bulb, candles were a primary source of light at night, assuring our ancestors didn't trip over the furniture at night.

Candles, in ancient Egypt, were an integral part of religious ceremonies and were used to pay homage to the various gods and goddesses worshiped at that time. The ancient people firmly held the belief that the flame they lit symbolized the never-ending light of the sun deity Ra, and they relied on candles to establish a spiritual connection with the divine and ask for guidance. The practitioners who engaged in candle magik in earlier times had a deep understanding of the significance of intention and visualization. They employed particular colors and symbols to align with their desired outcomes.

The practice of candle magik also played a significant role in ancient Greek and Roman cultures. The Greeks used candles to worship their gods, particularly in the form of votive offerings. These small candles were lit to show devotion and gratitude, and it was believed that the gods would grant their requests in return. People still use these small candles in much the same way, not only at home, but in churches.

In medieval Europe, candle magik became intertwined with witchcraft and the occult. During this time, candles were used not only in religious rituals but also in spells and enchantments. The era of tolerance towards witches lasted until the reign of James I, but unfortunately, things took a turn for the worse for them very quickly thereafter. Witches and sorcerers believed that the flame of a candle contained transformative energy that could be harnessed for various purposes, including love, healing, and protection.

As time went on, candle magik evolved and adapted to different cultures and belief systems. It became an integral part of various spiritual practices, including Wicca and other modern forms of witchcraft. Today, candle magik is widely practiced by those interested in the occult, witchcraft, and the metaphysical.

In contemporary candle magik, each color and type of candle holds specific meanings and properties. For example, red candles are often used in love and passion spells, while green candles are associated with abundance and prosperity. By combining the right candle color, intention, and ritual, practitioners can tap into the energy of the universe and manifest their desires.

Whether you are seeking love and relationships, healing and wellness, or spiritual enlightenment and guidance, candle magik offers a versatile and powerful tool to enhance your practice. By understanding its history and origins, you can deepen your connection to this ancient art and unlock the power within.

Candle Safety

In 1999, I had an unfortunate incident where a pillar candle I was burning spilled wax on the old ash in my empty fireplace, causing ignition. Since then, I have perfected my skills in safe candle burning.

I was working a multiple candle ritual, using plain 2" pillar-type candles, burned in my fireplace. That evening, I was outside with neighbors, our usual evening neighborhood gathering. I needed another glass of refreshment, so I went back inside from my garage. Upon entering the house, I was surprised to see a huge flame roaring out of the fireplace. I mean, it was actually roaring. The moment I noticed the fire, I acted fast and grabbed a bin of cat litter which I used with the fireplace shovel to extinguish the flames. To ensure that the living room was not engulfed in smoke, I opened the flue after putting out the fire.

That was a close call. I spent the next day trying to remove the black soot from the walls, and wound up having to repaint the entire living room.

After I'd cleaned up, I realized that I had left the paper sticker on the bottom of the candles, and these caught fire when the candle began to burn out. The flame, along with the melted wax pool below it, soaked the ashes in the fireplace. And up it went.

From that incident, I have developed a strict set of rules for burning my candles, and I suggest you pay careful attention.

The best possible place to burn a candle unattended is in a clean fireplace, with the candle in a solid metal holder, and all stickers removed. A glass prayer candle should also be placed into a solid fire resistant bowl, perhaps lined with sand. Second best, put it on a small piece of wooden or ceramic coaster.

Another good spot is inside a cold oven. You'll get some carbon soot on the top of the oven, but it's far safer than anywhere else if you don't have a fireplace.

You can also place the candle(s) in a bathtub, in the center, with any shower curtain pulled well away from it.

In a garage or basement, with a concrete floor, put the candles on the floor about 14 inches from all objects. I'd rather scrape up solid wax from the floor than rebuild a house.

Just check any fire department website and look for house or apartment fires caused by unattended candles. When burning an 18+ hour candle, it's not workable to keep a constant eye on it. A post appeared on one of my frequent social media groups a few years ago, detailing the tragic death of a fellow group member in a house fire. The fire was started by a candle that had been placed too close to the cloth of an altar, causing the entire house to be engulfed in flames.

Another risk is tying anything around a candle and burning it.

I have seen several spells and rituals which call for a ribbon or string to be tied around a candle or between candles and then burned. The risk here is that the item tied to the candle will soak up melted wax, then ignite. To low-key this, this will have a non-beneficial effect. What you do is use small chime candles and keep them in the same room with you until the candles are done.

The same goes for sprinkling herbs into a glass votive candle. The dried bits of plant material will soak up the wax, then ignite, and this risks causing the glass container to overheat, often in a concentrated spot, which then makes the glass break. Not only is it a mess, it's dangerous.

Burning the Candles

There are few rules when using candle magik. But the rules that exist are important.

Rules for Burning Candles:

1. Allow the candle to burn out completely. If it goes out, relight as soon as possible.

2. Never, ever blow out a candle. If you need to extinguish it, use a candle snuffer.

(Birthday candles? Don't really make a wish when blowing out the candles. Blowing out the candles tends to negate the wish happening. Which explains my childhood disappointments)

3. Dispose of all excess wax drippings by burying the wax. Never toss into the trash.

4. Never burn a green or gold candle with a red candle. This

combination will trigger excessive spending.

5. For holidays, when combining colors such as gold/green with red, just have the candles out, do not burn them.

As always, burn the candles safely. I can't emphasize this too much. You'll read that statement a lot in this book.

Sometimes, in online groups, especially groups for magik, someone will post a picture of a candle burning, and the pattern the wax made while burning. Then there'll be discussions about what is seen or what the patterns mean. Don't worry about any of that with this type of candle magik.

All you need to worry about is if the candle goes out. When this happens, simply carve the wax so that the wick is exposed again, and relight the candle.

CHAPTER TWO

Welcome to the world of candle magik, where the flickering flame holds the power to unlock your inner potential and manifest your desires. Whether you are new to witchcraft, the occult, or the realm of magik, this section will provide you with a solid foundation to delve into the enchanting world of candle magik.

Candles have a unique ability to absorb out intent, and release it over the period the candle burns. The color of the candle will also attract the energies associated with that color. Pink attracts (among other things) love and fulfilled wishes. Green or gold attracts prosperity and money, blue attracts healing, and white attracts peace and protection.

When setting an intent, it is important to focus on the result you wish, rather than the means to achieve it. For example, if you want to attract wealth, focus on the feeling of wealth rather than on the amount of money you wish to attract. Visualize yourself feeling wealthy and abundant while focusing on the emotions of abundance. Affirmations can be used to reinforce the intent, such as, "I am abundant and wealthy."

It is also important to use specific words when setting an intent. Visualize what you are asking for, and speak it out loud as you light the candle. For example, you could say, "I light this pink candle to attract love and fulfilled wishes into my life."

The scope of candle intent is not confined to establishing an intention; there is much more to it than that. Apart from its main use, it can be employed as a method of purifying an area, or conversely, as a means of imbuing it with positive energy. While the candle burns, one can set their intent by saying something like, "As this candle burns, I set my intention to cleanse this space of all negative energy." In a similar manner, you have the option to say the following words, "I infuse this space with positive energy and good vibes."

Use simple statements, because if you allow yourself to place a lot of conditions on the magik, it'll delay the actual magik. Simple statements help to keep the magik clean and efficient.

Candle magik rituals and spells have been practiced for centuries, tapping into the energy of fire and using the power of intention to create transformation. By understanding the basics of candle magik, you will learn how to harness this energy and direct it towards specific areas of your life.

So, let's explore the magik of candles!

Love and Relationships Candle Magic Rituals and Spells: Discover how to attract love, enhance existing relationships, and heal emotional wounds through the use of candle magik. Learn about the symbolism of different candle colors and how to infuse them with your intentions to manifest a more fulfilling love life.

Healing and Wellness Candle Magic Rituals and Spells: Explore the healing properties of candles and how they can promote physical, emotional, and spiritual well-being. Learn techniques to ease pain, release negative energy, and restore balance within yourself and others.

Prosperity and Abundance Candle Magic Rituals and Spells: Unleash the power of candle magik to manifest abundance, wealth, and financial stability. Discover rituals and spells that align with your goals and attract the prosperity and success you desire.

Protection and Cleansing Candle Magic Rituals and Spells: Learn how to create a sacred space and protect yourself from negative energies and influences. Explore rituals and spells that cleanse and purify your environment, promoting a sense of safety and harmony.

Manifestation and Law of Attraction Candle Magic Rituals and Spells: Tap into the universal law of attraction and learn how to manifest your dreams and desires through candle magik. Discover techniques to amplify your intentions and align yourself with the energy of abundance.

Spiritual Enlightenment and Guidance Candle Magic Rituals and Spells: Connect with your higher self and receive spiritual guidance through candle magik. Explore rituals and spells that open pathways to enlightenment, deepen your spiritual practice, and strengthen your intuition.

Career and Success Candle Magic Rituals and Spells: Utilize the power of candle magik to enhance your career, attract opportunities, and achieve success. Discover rituals and spells that align with your professional goals and help you manifest your desired outcomes.

Psychic Development and Intuition Candle Magic Rituals and Spells: Awaken your psychic abilities and expand your intuition through the practice of candle magik. Learn techniques to enhance your psychic senses and tap into the wisdom of the universe.

Self-Love and Confidence Candle Magic Rituals and Spells: Nurture self-love, boost confidence, and cultivate a positive self-image through candle magik. Discover rituals and spells that promote self-acceptance, inner strength, and a deep sense of worthiness.

Lunar and Celestial Energy Candle Magic Rituals and Spells: Harness the energy of the moon and celestial bodies to amplify the power of your candle magik. Explore rituals and spells that align with the phases of the moon and tap into the cosmic energies for manifestation and spiritual growth.

With a solid understanding of the basics of candle magik, you are now ready to embark on a journey of self-discovery, transformation, and manifestation. Embrace the power within and unlock the limitless possibilities that candle magik holds.

Understanding the Power and Symbolism of Candles

Candle magik is a powerful practice that has been used for centuries by those interested in witchcraft, the occult, and magik. The flame of a candle holds a deep symbolism, representing the element of fire and the transformational power it brings. In this section, we will explore the significance of candles in various aspects of life and delve into the different rituals and spells associated with them.

In this book, we will explore rituals and spells associated with spiritual enlightenment and guidance, career and success, psychic development and intuition, self-love and confidence, lunar and celestial energy, and much more. By understanding the power and symbolism of candles, you can unlock the hidden potential within yourself and create positive changes in all areas of your life. Join us as we journey into the world of candle magik and tap into the limitless possibilities it offers.

Whether you are a beginner or experienced practitioner, you will find something magical here. Open your heart and mind to the possibilities and be prepared to be enlightened!

Timing and Candle Magik

The power for the manifestation of a desire is gained through the utilization of specific astrological events in most forms of traditional magik. Symbols, chants, and various other rituals are integral components of these traditional magik practices. The belief in some traditions is that the power of magik is not inherent in the practitioner, but rather their ability to manipulate the natural forces of the universe to achieve their desired outcome. Magik is perceived differently across various traditions and cultures. In some, it is considered to be the power of the gods or other supernatural entities. Some magik systems, such as Chaos magik, dispenses with all timings.

With candle magik, it's simplified so that it only needs the timings associated with the lunar cycle to make it all work.

The lunar cycle is divided into two specific phases. Bring Cycle where you intend to bring something into your life, and the Release Cycle, where you intend to release something from your life.

Bring Cycle

The Bring Cycle is the phase of the lunar cycle where you focus on bringing something new into your life. This could be a new job, a new relationship, a new project, or any other desired outcome. During this phase, you focus on setting intentions and goals that you want to manifest in your life. You also take action steps to help bring these desires into reality. Action steps will depend on the subject of the ritual itself, such as getting out and about to mingle when wanting to attract a life partner, or apply for that job you desire.

Release Cycle

The Release Cycle is the phase of the lunar cycle where you focus on releasing something from your life. This could be an old habit, an outdated belief system, or anything else that is no longer serving you. During this phase, you focus on releasing old energies that may be holding you back and creating space for new opportunities. You also use this time to reflect on your progress and evaluate how you can improve.

The calculation of each phase is in sync with the New Moon and Full Moon. You may also work magik on the actual time of the Full or New Moon, depending on your needs.

I have created a table (at the end of this book) to assist you in calculating when to work rituals in each cycle. There is a bit of leeway, but not much. If you are working during the Bring Cycle, make sure to begin a few hours after the New Moon, and make sure the ritual candles are finished by the time the new cycle begins. Decades of working candle magik has shown me the power of working within these cycles.

The old book I originally owned suggested it was okay to allow a candle that started during the Bring phase to continue into the Release phase, but my own experiences indicate this isn't a good practice.

Also, during the rituals that follow, make sure to allow the candles to burn completely, and just know that a 7-day candle should not be started if it won't finish by the start of the next cycle. If you must start a 7-day candle when you won't be able to finish it, be sure to snuff it out and relight it the next time you're able to do the ritual. Most 7-day candles will burn approximately 4 to 5 days.

CHAPTER THREE

Tools and Supplies

As with all magik, having the right tools and supplies is crucial for successful rituals and spells. Whether you are a seasoned practitioner or a beginner exploring the world of magik, understanding the essential items needed for candle magik will empower and enhance your practice. This section will guide you through the must-have tools and supplies, ensuring you are well-equipped to unlock the power within.

Finding Candles

Years ago, my favorite store to find candles locally was a major chain craft store. One, in particular, would stock just about every size and shape I'd ever want. I grew fond of using a type they called a "carriage" candle. In deep green, pink, yellow, and even in gold.

Recently, this same store chain appears to have reduced their stock. Most of the time, I find empty shelves in the candle department. So I turned to other types of candles, ones that are easy to locate.

Online, I found a company who sells smaller votive candles, in six-packs. These glass candles are 3-inches wide by about 6-inches tall, and last around eighteen hours. They use soy and are unscented.

Search for "Haoson Unscented Green Candles" to locate the ones I've been using while writing this book. Alternatively, you might find some "7-day" candles local to you, which is better than buying them online. When I have been able to find one, they're often under $2.00 (US).

Another option is air freshener candles. I have found the shorter, pine scented candles in glass holders to be very useful. Once the candle itself is done, you can clean up the glass holder, which is often a solid candle holder.

You can also use pillar candles, anything wider than 2 inches (5 cm) are good. The bigger, the longer a candle will burn. Votive candles in glass holders are prefect because they will not spill wax while burning (unless the glass breaks) and burn longer. A pillar candle, if burned where it's hit by even the slightest of drafts, will begin to spill wax and lose its effectiveness as all the wax isn't being used.

Don't bother with candles that are already charged with energy, as they tend to lose their charge when shipped, owing to the handling of those who pack and unpack trucks and the local delivery personnel. Just look for the best candle to fit the job. Unless you can source such candles locally to you.

Many of the rituals will call for multiple candles, so be prepared to collect lots of glass candle holders. Many, especially the smaller ones, can be reused. I will line the bottom with aluminum foil, hit the bottom of the candle with a lighter so that melted wax drips onto the foil, and then I put the candle down into the wax quickly, so that it sticks to the candle. It also makes for fast clean-up.

Reversing Candles

In some of my rituals, you will need to start with a reversing candle, especially with income rituals. For example, to reverse negative energy, grab a small red candle, like a chime candle or small pillar candle. Turn it upside down, flipping it. Cut the bottom so that it's flat, then carve the new top to expose the wick.

You can buy pre-made reversing candles, such as a black and red, or black and green. These still need to be flipped and cut, but work wonderfully.

Colors: The significance of different colors cannot be overstated, as each color holds unique energies that can positively impact one's well-being, thereby making it essential to have a diverse collection of candles. There are several colors that symbolize different meanings, such as red which symbolizes love and passion, and often red symbolizes negativity energy (so be careful), green which signifies prosperity and abundance, white which represents purity and cleansing, and many others. In order to achieve the best possible results, it is recommended that you carefully select candles that align with your desired outcome.

In a pinch, you can work magik with just white candles. I do this all the time. I'll need an orange candle for a road clearing ritual, but none are on hand. I'll create a sigil (sigils are covered in my High Magik Series and are abstract symbols that represent my desired outcome). With the sigil, I will draw with a paint pen on the white candle. Then I'll set the intention, and the candle will work as if it's an orange candle. You can also use various herbs, oils, and stones with the white candle to add more power to the magik. For example, if I were using the white candle for a road opening spell, I might anoint it with rosemary oil, sprinkle it with salt, and place a piece of carnelian in front of it.

Candle Holders: To safely burn your candles, invest in sturdy candle holders that suit your style and preferences. From elegant glass holders to rustic metal ones, find the perfect fit for your rituals and spells. I have found many nice holders at second-hand shops (in the US, Goodwill, etc) Remember, safety is paramount, so ensure the candle holders are stable and can withstand the heat of the flame. Earlier, I mentioned the small air freshener candles, and the glass they come in are suitable to hold smaller (less and 1" diameter) candles once cleaned up.

Essential Oils: Enhance the power of your candle magik with essential oils. These potent extracts hold specific properties that can amplify your intentions. Lavender for relaxation, rose for love, eucalyptus for healing – the possibilities are endless. Invest in high-quality essential oils and use them to anoint your candles before each ritual or spell.

Herbs and Crystals: Incorporating herbs and crystals into your candle magik adds an extra layer of energy and intention. Research the properties of different herbs and crystals to find those that align with your desired outcomes. For love and relationships, rose quartz and dried rose petals are ideal, while for protection and cleansing, black tourmaline and sage leaves are recommended. Abre Camino is a herb I use a lot with road opener rituals.

In traditional magik, crystals also represent the element "Earth". They will soak up energy and later broadcast that energy. I advise to always cleanse your crystals in salt every so often, to reset them. I place some coarse pickling salt into a zip-lock bag, then drop in the crystal, and allow it to set a few days to a week. Then it's sufficiently cleared and ready to be used again.

Black Salt: A standard for banishing candles. It's a simple mixture of charred herbs or a piece of charcoal crushed to a powder, then mixed with table salt. Set this aside and only use it with your candles.

To use: take a drop of a neutral oil (mineral oil, almond oil, or magik oil) and coat the candle. Then lightly sprinkle the black salt onto the candle.

Incense or Herb Bundles: Clearing the energy before and after your candle magik rituals is essential. Burn incense or purifying herb bundles to purify the space and create a sacred atmosphere. Frankincense, sandalwood, and sage are popular choices, but feel free to explore different scents that resonate with you. I have found frankincense to work the best, followed by sandalwood. Sage is good if you have nothing else.

With all herbs used on or in candles, try to make sure they are finely powdered, using a spice grinder. This way, when coating the candle (or sprinkling into a 7-day votive candle) you won't have any issues with larger bits of plant material becoming a second wick and causing issues while the candle burns.

Mirrors: The use of small mirrors while burning a candle will reflect its energy and effectively double the magik. Like two-for-one, which explains why I have a collection of small, 3" square mirrors laying in my altar area.

This list provides a solid foundation for your candle magik practice. As you dive deeper into specific niches within candle magik, such as love and relationships, healing and wellness, or prosperity and abundance, you may discover additional tools and supplies that align with those intentions. Remember, your magikal journey is unique, so trust your intuition and let it guide you to the tools and supplies that will enhance your practice and unlock the power within.

Setting Up Your Sacred Space for Rituals

Although creating a sacred space for your candle magik rituals is not fully needed, it does set the stage for your intentions and allows you to connect with the energy of the universe. Whether you are a beginner or an experienced practitioner, having a dedicated space for your rituals will enhance the power of your spells. In this section, we will explore the key elements of setting up your sacred space for rituals.

Foremost, find a space in your home that feels comfortable and private. This could be a corner of your bedroom, a spare room, or even an outdoor area. The important thing is that it is a place where you can be undisturbed during your rituals.

My current space is in my basement. I used to work in my garage, and before that, I had a temporary space in my bedroom. Use what you have, even if it's temporary. Just remember, the whole goal of using candle magik is to have the candles burning, with no one knowing you are working magik. Make it easy.

Once you have chosen your space, it's time to cleanse and purify it. This can be done by smudging with sage or using other purifying herbs such as lavender or rosemary. Visualize any negative energy being cleared away, making space for positive energy to flow.

Next, consider the décor of your sacred space. Choose items that resonate with your intentions and the specific type of candle magik you are practicing. For love and relationships, you might include symbols of love, such as hearts or roses. For healing and wellness, incorporate soothing colors and natural elements like crystals or plants. The key is to create an atmosphere that aligns with your desired outcomes.

A central focus of your sacred space should be your altar. This is where you will perform your rituals and place your candles. Choose a table or surface that is sturdy and large enough to hold your tools and offerings. Decorate your altar with meaningful objects, such as statues, pictures, or symbols that represent the areas of candle magik you are working with.

Consider the lighting in your sacred space. Soft, warm lighting from candles or fairy lights can create a calming and magical ambiance. You may also want to include a reading or meditation corner with a comfortable chair or cushions where you can sit and reflect.

Finally, it is important to create a routine and establish boundaries for your sacred space. Set aside specific times for your rituals and ensure that you will not be disturbed during this time. This will allow you to fully immerse yourself in the energy of your practice.

By creating a dedicated and sacred space for your candle magik rituals, you are opening the door to the infinite possibilities of the universe. Embrace the power within you and let your intentions manifest through the art of candle magik.

CHAPTER FOUR

Love and Relationships

One area of magik I used to work a lot was Love and Sex magik, honestly, I did this quite a bit when I was younger. I can report that this works, and works well, as long as you can let go of the outcomes. However, understand the power of this type of magik and that it can be the most difficult, as you are attempting to make someone possibly act against their own internal compass.

When working with Love and Sex magik, the most important thing is to be sure that you are doing so ethically and responsibly. When working with this type of magik, it is also important to be aware of the consequences of your actions. It is not something to be taken lightly or used without thought. I speak from experience here. While some worked out well, others became a nightmare, both for me and later for the woman. Be sure to think through everything that you do and the consequences of your actions before you begin. A rebound of the magik can occur, making you feel many, many times worse afterwards. It was a hard-learned lesson for me. As I also do work for others, I have seen clients also learn this lesson as well. So please be aware and responsible when working with this type of magik.

When attempting to use Love and Sex magik, it is important to keep several things in mind. First, be sure that your intentions are clear and that you are not trying to manipulate anyone or anything. Second, be sure to keep your energy focused on the positive outcome that you are trying to create and not on the negative. Third, be sure to take responsibility for the consequences of your actions. Lastly, be sure to be respectful of the person you are working with and to not push too hard.

Love and Sex magik can be a powerful tool, but it is important to remember to use it responsibly and ethically.

In this chapter, we will explore the art of attracting love and romance through candle magik rituals and spells. Whether you are looking to ignite the passion in an existing relationship or find a soul-mate, these techniques can help you align your energy with the vibrations of love.

First, it is crucial to choose the right candles for your love and romance rituals. Red and pink candles are commonly associated with affection, passion, and love. You may also consider using a combination of candles that correspond to specific intentions, such as rose (bright pale pink) for self-love or lavender for attracting a soul-mate.

Once you have selected your candles, it is essential to cleanse and charge them with your intent. This can be done by holding the candle in your hands, visualizing your desired outcome, and infusing it with loving energy. You may also anoint the candles with oils or herbs that resonate with love, such as rose oil or jasmine petals.

Next, set the mood for your ritual. This can be as simple as dimming the lights, playing soft music, and setting up a comfortable altar. You may choose to incorporate love-related symbols, such as hearts or images of deities associated with love, such as Aphrodite or Freya.

During the ritual, focus your thoughts and emotions on the love and romance you wish to attract. Light the candles and visualize the energy of love emanating from them, surrounding you and filling your space. You may recite affirmations or chants that resonate with your intention, expressing gratitude for the love that is coming into your life.

After the ritual, it is essential to release attachment to the outcome and trust in the universe's timing. Remember that candle magik is a form of energy work, and results may manifest in unexpected ways or at unexpected times. Stay open to the possibilities and be receptive to the love that is flowing towards you.

Remember to approach these rituals with love, gratitude, and an open heart, and trust in the universal forces conspiring to bring love into your life.

Healing a Broken Heart and Emotional Wounds

Candle magik, which is an ancient practice, holds within it a powerful tool that can be used to heal emotional wounds and mending a broken heart. Our emotions are intricate threads that weave through our existence, and when they become frayed or torn, it can leave us feeling lost and vulnerable. However, with the art of candle magik, we have the ability to harness the power within and start a transformative healing process.

A common issue with many people seeking a new relationship is healing the wounds of a past relationship. I know from counseling hundreds of people that when there is still pain and hurt from a previous relationship, there is little room for a new lover or relationship. Before one can move on, the past must be let go, or you risk more heartache and pain. This healing will open you up for a new love.

When it comes to healing a broken heart, the flickering flame of a candle can serve as a guiding light towards inner peace and emotional restoration. By creating a sacred space and selecting the appropriate candles, we can embark on a journey of self-discovery and healing.

One ritual that can aid in this process is the 'Heart Healing Ritual.' Begin by lighting a pink or pale blue candle, symbolizing love and compassion. Take a moment to connect with your emotions and acknowledge the pain you are experiencing. As the flame dances, visualize it gently caressing your wounded heart, soothing and healing the hurt. Feel the warmth and love emanating from the candle, enveloping you in a comforting embrace.

As the candle burns, you may choose to write down your feelings on a piece of paper, releasing them into the flame as an act of letting go. Alternatively, you can place healing crystals, such as rose quartz or amethyst, around the candle to amplify the energetic healing properties.

Repeat this ritual as often as needed during the bring cycle, allowing the candle's flame to serve as a constant reminder of your commitment to healing. Over time, you will notice the transformative power of candle magik as it gradually mends the broken pieces of your heart, bringing forth emotional wholeness and inner strength.

Remember, healing is a process, and everyone's journey is unique. Be patient and gentle with yourself as you embark on this path of emotional healing. The power of candle magik is here to support and guide you, providing solace and rejuvenation during your time of need.

By embracing the art of candle magik, you can tap into the hidden depths of your emotions, heal your heart, and find the strength to move forward. Allow the flame to illuminate your path towards emotional wellness and discover the transformative power of candle magik in healing your broken heart.

Strengthening and Deepening Existing Relationships

In the realm of candle magic, relationships hold a special place. Whether it is a romantic partnership, a friendship, or a familial bond, the connections we have with others shape our lives in profound ways. This section delves into the art of strengthening and deepening existing relationships through the simple use of candle magic.

By harnessing the energy of fire and the symbolism of candles, we can create powerful spells to nurture and strengthen the bonds we share with others.

Whether you are seeking to attract new love or kindle the flame in an existing relationship, candle magic can be a potent tool. Explore rituals to invoke passion, promote harmony, and increase intimacy in your romantic connections. Learn how to infuse your love life with the energy of the universe, allowing your relationships to flourish and grow.

Relationships can sometimes bear the weight of emotional wounds and hardships. Discover candle magic rituals and spells to heal past traumas, release negative energy, and restore balance within yourself and your connections with others. Create a sacred space of healing and wellness that supports the growth and transformation of your relationships.

When our relationships are strong and thriving, they can become a catalyst for prosperity and abundance. By aligning your relationships with the energy of abundance, you can create a supportive environment for the manifestation of your dreams.

Just as relationships can bring joy, they can also encounter challenges and negative influences. Learn how to use candle magic to protect your relationships from external harm and cleanse them of any negative energies that may be hindering their growth. Research and create your own rituals to create a shield of love and light around your connections, fostering a safe and harmonious space for growth.

In the art of candle magic, relationships are elevated to a sacred realm. By incorporating candle magic rituals and spells into your daily practice, you can deepen and strengthen the bonds you share with others. Allow the flame of your intentions to burn brightly, illuminating the path to love, healing, abundance, and spiritual enlightenment within your relationships.

Enhancing Passion and Intimacy in Relationships

In the realm of love and relationships, passion and intimacy are vital ingredients for a fulfilling and enduring connection. Candle magic can be a powerful tool to enhance and strengthen these aspects, allowing you to deepen your bond and create a more vibrant and intimate relationship.

Passion is the fire that ignites the soul, and candle magic can help stoke those flames. Begin by selecting a red or pink candle, symbolizing love and desire. Carve both your names and a heart into the wax, infusing it with your intention for heightened passion. Light the candle and visualize the flames representing the passion you wish to kindle in your relationship. As the candle burns, allow the energy to envelop you both, bringing forth a renewed sense of desire and ardor.

Intimacy is the foundation of any successful relationship, and candle magic can help foster a deeper connection between partners. Choose a white or blue candle, signifying purity and communication. Write down your deepest feelings and desires for a more intimate connection. Place the paper beneath the candle and light it, allowing the flame to transfer your intentions into the universe. As the candle burns, communicate openly and honestly with your partner, sharing your thoughts and vulnerabilities. This ritual will help create a safe space for emotional and physical intimacy to flourish.

For added power, use a photograph of your partner, or even a strand of their hair, wrapped with your hair, then tied around the candle.

As the sparks of passion and intimacy grow, it is essential to maintain a harmonious and balanced relationship. Incorporate healing and wellness candle magic rituals into your routine. Use green candles to represent healing and abundance. Light the candle and visualize any wounds or past traumas being cleansed and transformed into love and compassion. This ritual will help cultivate a healthy and supportive environment for your relationship to thrive.

Remember, the key to a successful relationship lies in nurturing it continuously. By incorporating candle magic rituals into your love and relationship practices, you can create a stronger, more passionate, and intimate connection. Explore the diverse range of candle magic rituals and spells in this book to unlock the power within and manifest a love that transcends all boundaries.

Releasing Negative Relationship Patterns

Sometimes, in even the best loving relationships, negative patterns can emerge and often hinder our ability to find true happiness and fulfillment. These patterns can stem from past traumas, childhood experiences, or even societal conditioning. However, with the power of candle magic, we can release these negative relationship patterns and pave the way for healthier and more loving connections.

Candle magic rituals and spells provide a powerful tool for transformation and healing. By harnessing the energy of candles, we can access the deep recesses of our subconscious mind and break free from negative relationship patterns that no longer serve us.

To begin this journey of releasing negative relationship patterns, it is important to first identify and acknowledge these patterns. Reflect on past relationships and take note of any recurring themes or behaviors that have caused pain or dissatisfaction. This self-reflection is a crucial step in understanding the root causes of these patterns.

Once you have identified the negative relationship patterns, it is time to design a candle magic ritual to release them. Start by selecting a candle color that resonates with your intention. For releasing negative patterns, black or dark blue candles are often used. However, trust your intuition and choose a color that feels right for you.

During the ritual, light the candle and focus your intention on releasing the negative relationship patterns. Visualize these patterns dissipating and being replaced by positive, loving energy. You can also incorporate affirmations or mantras into your ritual to reinforce your intention.

As the candle burns, imagine the flame consuming and transmuting the negative patterns. Feel a sense of liberation and freedom as you let go of the past and make space for healthier relationships to enter your life. Remember to express gratitude for the lessons learned from these negative patterns, as they have ultimately led you to this moment of growth and transformation.

Releasing negative relationship patterns through candle magic is a continuous process. It requires dedication, self-reflection, and a willingness to let go. However, by incorporating candle magic rituals into your spiritual practice, you can break free from the chains of negative patterns and create a future filled with love, joy, and fulfilling relationships. Trust in the power of candle magic and the transformative energy it holds to unlock the true potential within you.

10-day Magik Sequence for Attracting Love

This is a simple, multiple day ritual, which can be easily worked in plain sight.

Make sure to have a safe space for the candle burning, and that your ritual space is clear, and has been charged as previously instructed. Perhaps, use the emotional healing ritual before using this ritual to make sure you are emotionally healthy for a new relationship.

You will need 10 (ten) pink candles. Small chime candles work great for this, as well as the 7-day votive candles. Chime candles will burn for less than an hour, but, ironically, the 7-day candles usually only burn for 4 days. You can also purchase pink taper candles which will burn for several hours. Make sure to begin as early in the bring cycle as possible.

Hold each candle and set your intention to draw love to you. Hold this and do some visualization where you meet the person of your dreams. Imagine what they look like, how they make you feel, and the things you do together. Then, take a deep breath and allow yourself to let it go.

Once you have set your intention, light the candles and focus on the flame. Take a few moments to reflect on the love that you wish to draw into your life. Visualize this love entering your life and wrapping you up in their warmth and comfort.

Take a few moments to focus on the feeling of love and the possibilities that can come from it. Feel the love in your heart and the joy that it brings.

Release your intention into the Universe and trust that it will be answered with perfect timing.

Repeat this for 10 days.

At the end of the 10-days, carefully dispose of any remaining candle wax by burying the wax in the ground. If you used glass votive candles, recycle the containers.

3-day Magik Sequence for Inflaming Desire

Another simple ritual sequence. This ritual uses red candles, and I recommend the medium taper candles, or 1" pillar candles.

As you have been advised previously, make sure to burn these candles in a safe manner, making sure your altar space is clean and free of clutter.

Start this during the Bring Cycle and make sure you can finish at least one day prior to the start of a Release cycle. Refer to the tables at the end of the book for the exact dates and times.

Red candles are for passion, and this ritual is designed to reignite that initial flame of passion after a relationship has shifted into a long-term, but boring, period.

Hold each candle and set your intention to draw your partner passionately to you. Hold this and do some visualization where you and your partner are enjoying deep, passionate love. Then, take a deep breath and allow yourself to let it go.

Once you have set your intention, light the candles and focus on the flame. Take a few moments to reflect on the passion that you wish to draw into your life. Visualize your partner passionately wrapping you up in his/her arms up, and this effect on you.

Take a few moments to focus on the feeling of passion returning and the possibilities that can come from it. Feel the love in your heart and the joy that it brings.

Release your intention into the Universe and trust that it will be answered with perfect timing, so put it out of your mind. Never ask "when", as that usually slows the magik.

Repeat this for 3 days.

At the end of the 3-days, carefully dispose of any remaining candle wax by burying the wax in the ground. If you used glass votive candles, recycle the containers.

CHAPTER FIVE

Rituals and Spells for Healing and Wellness

With all magik, the power to heal and nurture our physical bodies is within our grasp. By harnessing the energy and symbolism of candles, we can unlock the potential for physical healing and enhance our overall wellbeing. This section explores the various rituals and spells that focus on promoting physical healing and restoring balance to the body.

One of the fundamental aspects of candle magic for physical healing is the use of color. Each color carries unique vibrations that resonate with different aspects of our physical and energetic bodies. For example, green candles are commonly associated with physical healing and rejuvenation, while blue candles can help soothe pain and promote calmness. By choosing the appropriate color for your specific needs, you can amplify the desired healing effects.

A simple ritual for physical healing involves creating a sacred space and choosing a candle that resonates with your intentions. Begin by cleansing your space and yourself, using purification rituals such as smudging or visualizing white light surrounding you. Light the selected candle and focus your intention on the areas of your body that require healing. Visualize the healing energy flowing into those areas, bringing relief and restoration. You can also incorporate affirmations or chants that affirm your intentions for physical healing.

Some good, Law of Attraction type of affirmations are (copy these and print them out):

"I am grateful for the natural healing power within my body, and I trust it to restore me to perfect health."

"Every day, in every way, I am getting healthier and stronger."

"I release any negativity from my body and embrace healing energy in every cell."

"I am surrounded by loving and supportive energy that aids in my complete healing."

"My body knows how to heal itself, and I allow it to do so effortlessly."

"I am open to receiving healing energy from the universe, and I am worthy of vibrant health."

"I attract and focus on positive thoughts that contribute to my overall well-being."

"My mind, body, and spirit are in perfect harmony, promoting healing and balance."

"I am resilient, and my body has an amazing ability to bounce back to optimal health."

"Every breath I take fills my body with healing energy, restoring me to wholeness."

Another powerful tool in promoting physical wellbeing through candle magic is the use of essential oils. These oils possess potent healing properties that can be harnessed when combined with the energy of candles. For example, lavender oil is known for its calming and pain-relieving effects, while eucalyptus oil can aid in respiratory health. By anointing your candle with the appropriate essential oil, you can enhance the healing properties of your ritual.

Additionally, incorporating crystals into your candle magic rituals can further amplify the healing energy. Crystals such as amethyst, clear quartz, and rose quartz are particularly beneficial for physical healing and overall wellbeing. Place these crystals near your candle or hold them in your hands while performing the ritual to harness their healing vibrations.

Remember, physical healing is a holistic process that involves not only the body but also the mind and spirit. By integrating candle magic rituals into your wellness routine, you can align these aspects and promote overall balance and vitality.

The practice of candle magik can be a powerful and transformative tool that facilitates emotional healing and release. Through the art of candle magic, which involves combining the energy of candles with intention, visualization, and ritual, we can tap into the innate power within ourselves that enables us to heal emotional wounds, release past traumas, and make room for personal growth and transformation.

The art of candle magik has been revered for centuries because of its uncanny ability to connect us with the spiritual energies and elemental forces present in our surroundings. By using candles in a focused and intentional way, we can harness their power as conduits to help us direct our energy towards manifesting our desires. When it comes to emotional healing, candles can provide a safe and sacred environment that allows us to delve into our emotions, work through them, and ultimately let them go.

To begin your emotional healing and release journey, it is crucial to create a sacred space that promotes relaxation and introspection. Find a quiet corner of your home where you can light your candle and sit in stillness. Take a few deep breaths, allowing yourself to fully arrive in the present moment.

Choose a candle color that resonates with the emotions you wish to heal or release. For example, blue candles are often associated with calmness and tranquility, while pink candles symbolize love and compassion. As you light the candle, set your intention for emotional healing and release. Visualize the flickering flame as a representation of the emotions you wish to release, gently burning away the pain and hurt.

Run this ritual during the Release Cycle, as this is the perfect phase for releasing internal emotional baggage.

As the candle burns, you may choose to engage in journaling or meditation practices. Journaling allows you to explore and process your emotions, while meditation helps you cultivate a sense of inner peace and clarity. My favorite meditation is the simple "mindless meditation", where you allow yourself to simply "be in the moment". Trust your intuition and allow the candle's energy to guide you towards the healing practices that resonate with your needs.

Throughout your emotional healing and release ritual, remember to be kind and gentle with yourself. Emotions can be complex and may require time and patience to fully heal. Allow the candle's energy to support you in this process, knowing that each flame represents the transformative power within you.

By embracing the practice of emotional healing and release with candle magik, you can tap into the deep well of wisdom and strength within yourself. As you grow in your journey, you will find that candle magik becomes a powerful tool for self-discovery, healing, and personal transformation.

Enhancing Mental Clarity and Focus

In the realm of candle magik, the power to enhance mental clarity and focus is within your reach. The flickering flame and enchanting aromas of candles can stimulate your senses, creating a sacred space where you can unlock the potential of your mind. Whether you're a seasoned witch, an occult enthusiast, or simply curious about the mystic arts, this section will delve into the secrets of enhancing mental clarity and focus through candle magik.

Candle magik rituals and spells have been used for centuries to harness the energy of fire and channel it towards specific intentions. By incorporating specific herbs, colors, and symbols into your candle rituals, you can create a powerful atmosphere that aligns your thoughts and enhances mental acuity.

If you are looking to better your concentration, memory, or problem-solving skills, incorporating candle magik into your routine can provide you with the assistance you need on your journey towards progress. The first step in this process is to carefully choose a candle that aligns with the specific outcome you hope to achieve. When it comes to candle colors, blue candles are often associated with enhancing mental abilities, which means that they can be a great choice if you want to improve your cognitive function. On the other hand, purple candles promote spiritual insight and wisdom, making them an ideal choice for those who are interested in exploring their spirituality.

Once you have chosen your candle, infuse it with a blend of herbs and oils known for their cognitive-enhancing properties. Rosemary, lavender, and peppermint are excellent choices for stimulating mental clarity and focus. As you light the candle, visualize a bright, clear light enveloping your mind, dissolving any mental fog or distractions.

To deepen the effectiveness of your ritual, consider incorporating meditation and affirmations. By quieting the mind and focusing on positive thoughts and intentions, you can further enhance your mental clarity and focus. Repeat empowering affirmations such as "My mind is sharp and focused" or "I am fully present and in control of my thoughts."

Remember, candle magik is a personal journey, and the key to success lies in your intention and belief. Trust in the flame's power, and allow it to guide you towards heightened mental clarity and focus. With practice and dedication, you will unlock the true potential of your mind, achieving a state of heightened awareness and mental prowess.

Explore the vast realm of candle magik, and witness the transformative power it holds. From love and relationships to career and success, candle magik rituals and spells can be tailored to suit your specific needs and desires. Embrace the enchantment of the candle flame, and let it illuminate your path towards enhanced mental clarity and focus.

Boosting Energy and Vitality

The power to enhance our energy and vitality lies within our grasp when using any magik, and candle magik is no exception. By tapping into the mystical properties of candles and combining them with focused intention, we can invigorate our bodies and spirits, infusing them with a renewed sense of life force and enthusiasm. Regardless of whether you have been practicing for a long time or are just starting out on your journey in the mystical realm of witchcraft and magik, the comprehensive rituals and spells outlined in this chapter are designed to assist you in channeling the exact energy and vitality that you require.

Candle magik rituals and spells offer a unique approach to boosting energy and vitality. When we choose candles with particular colors and scents, we are essentially aligning ourselves with the elements and energies that are known to promote vitality and vigor, and this can have a significant impact on our overall well-being. For instance, red candles symbolize passion and strength, while orange candles represent creativity and enthusiasm. Incorporating these candles into your rituals and spells can help ignite the fire within you, giving you the energy to tackle any challenge that comes your way.

Love rituals or spells can also play a significant role in boosting energy and vitality. When we are in love and surrounded by positive relationships, our energy levels naturally increase. By utilizing candles associated with love and relationships, such as pink or white candles, we can attract and strengthen these connections, infusing us with the vibrant energy of love.

If you are looking for ways to increase your energy and vitality, you might want to consider incorporating healing rituals into your routine as they have been found to be a powerful tool. By focusing our intentions on healing and well-being, and utilizing candles with healing properties such as green or blue candles, we can tap into the restorative energies of the universe. These rituals and spells can help rejuvenate our bodies, minds, and spirits, promoting overall vitality and vitality.

Being financially stable and abundant has a direct impact on our sense of security and well-being, which in turn fuels our energy levels and motivates us to strive for more success. If we incorporate candles that are associated with prosperity and abundance, such as gold or green candles, into our rituals and spells, it is believed that we can attract and manifest the energy of abundance into our lives.

Also, by purging negative energies and protecting ourselves from harm, we can create a safe and sacred space to thrive. Black or white candles are commonly used for protection and cleansing rituals, helping us to release stagnant energy and restore balance within ourselves. More on this later on.

By engaging in spiritual rituals, individuals can tap into a unique approach to increase their energy and vitality. By establishing a connection with higher realms, which can be achieved through various spiritual practices, such as meditation, prayer, or ritual, and by seeking guidance from spiritual entities, such as angels, spirit guides, or ancestors, we can tap into a wellspring of energy and wisdom that can help us navigate our lives with greater clarity and purpose. Purple or white candles are commonly used for spiritual enlightenment and guidance rituals, helping us to access our inner power and divine connection.

The final thoughts on this chapter are that the rituals and spells mentioned here offer a wide range of ways to boost energy and vitality, each with its unique approach and advantages. Whether you are seeking to ignite your passion, attract love and abundance, heal and cleanse, manifest your desires, find spiritual guidance, achieve career success, enhance your psychic abilities, or cultivate self-love and confidence, candle magik can be a powerful tool. By combining the right candles, colors, and intention, you can tap into the energies that promote energy and vitality, unlocking your true potential within the realm of witchcraft and magik.

Protection and Banishing Negative Energies

In order to effectively work any magik, it is crucial to prioritize both protection and the banishing of negative energies. Throughout my time practicing the craft, I have encountered countless negative energies I'd rather forget. In this section, I will delve into various rituals and spells that can be used to shield ourselves and our surroundings from negativity, ensuring a safe and harmonious environment.

To begin, it is essential to cleanse and purify the space before conducting any protection rituals. This can be achieved by lighting a white candle and allowing its flame to burn away any lingering negative energies. Visualize the light from the candle spreading throughout the room, dispelling darkness and negativity.

Once the space is cleansed, we can proceed with banishing spells. One effective method is the use of a black candle, which represents absorbing and transmuting negative energies. Carve protective symbols or words onto the candle, such as pentagrams or the word "banish," to enhance its power. As the candle burns, imagine all negativity being drawn into the flame and dissipated, leaving only positivity in its wake.

Another powerful technique is the creation of a protection talisman using a white candle. Begin by anointing the candle with protective oils, such as cedarwood or frankincense, while focusing on your intent for protection. Light the candle and visualize a shield of white light surrounding you, warding off any negative influences. As you hold the candle, infuse it with your energy and intention, declaring your desire for protection. Carry the candle with you or place it in a prominent location as a constant reminder of your shield.

For those seeking protection specifically in love and relationships, a pink candle can be used. Similar to the previous rituals, anoint the candle with oils associated with love, such as rose or jasmine. Visualize a bubble of loving energy surrounding you and your partner, shielding your relationship from any negativity or harm. With each candle ritual, remember to state your intentions clearly and visualize the desired outcome.

Remember this, if nothing else from this chapter, that protection and banishing negative energies are paramount in the practice of candle magic. By incorporating these rituals and spells into your craft, you can create a sanctuary free from negativity and cultivate a harmonious environment. Whether it is shielding yourself, your relationships, or your space, candle magic is a potent tool for protection and banishing unwanted energies. Stay vigilant, stay protected, and unlock the power within.

Healing Sequence

What good does it do to manifest wealth or love if you're not healthy enough to enjoy it? This simple ritual sequence will help make you healthy.

One thing to remember, this ritual will not take the place of regular doctor visits. The way this magik works is by implanting within you the desire to get health, and to magically draw to you the tools and resources to maintain your health. A good example is when one of my students summoned the Grecian God Apollo (High Magik) to help her heal her son. What happened was that Apollo made sure the doctors found a viable transplant organ quickly. That was how the young man was healed. It wasn't some mysterious blue light orb zapping the kid with energy; it was directing the doctors and the transplant teams to the right donor.

General Healing

For general healing, we'll use standard blue candles. These can be the regular tapers, some solid 1" pillars, or the large votive candles in glass.

This is a three-day ritual, so buy three candles. You can buy more, if you choose, but at least three.

Beginning on a Sunday or Thursday, after the Bring cycle has begun, light the first candle.

Then light one candle a day for the following two days. For example, start on the Sunday, then Monday and finally Tuesday.

As with the other rituals, once you are finished, remove the melted wax and residue and bury it in the ground somewhere. If using the glass candles, simply recycle the containers.

General Healing Ritual Two (High Magik Style)

1. Begin by lighting a white candle, and calling in the four archangels of healing (Raphael, Michael, Gabriel, and Uriel). Ask them to help you with your healing journey.

2. Visualize your body in perfect health. See the organs functioning properly, and the energy in your body balanced and flowing freely.

3. Imagine that the archangels are pouring healing energy into your body. Picture a white light entering your body and filling every cell with energy.

4. Speak a mantra of healing. This can be something as simple as "I am healthy. I am whole. I am healed." Repeat this mantra three times.

5. Give thanks to the archangels for their assistance.

6. Blow out the candle and spend a few moments in meditation, focusing on your health and wellbeing.

7. Spend the next few days or weeks consciously engaging in activities that promote health and wellbeing. This can include eating nutritious foods, exercising, getting enough sleep, and engaging in activities that bring joy and peace.

This simple healing ritual sequence can help you take charge of your health, and to manifest the health and vitality that you desire

Healthy Lifestyle

A healthy lifestyle is important in living a fulfilling life. It's hard to live a life of abundance without a healthy lifestyle, because what good does it do to have a nice cash flow, but be too ill to enjoy it?

A lot of this ritual is in the mold of "Psychological Magik" where magik is used to nudge our subconscious into line, reprogramming our unhealthy habits.

What you do is up to you, but here's some helpful hints.

Use a pink candle for meditation, and while gazing at the candle, repeat a mantra (out loud or under your breath).

You can use any of the following mantras, or make up your own.

"My body is a temple, and I will treat it with love and respect."

"I nourish my body with wholesome foods that fuel my mind and soul."

"I am committed to regular exercise, and each step brings me closer to my best self."

"Health is my priority, and I make choices that support my well-being."

"I release stress and negativity, embracing peace and tranquility in my life."

"Every day is an opportunity to make progress towards a healthier me."

"I am in control of my habits, and I choose ones that serve my health."

"I listen to my body's needs and give it the rest and care it deserves."

"Small, consistent steps lead to significant and lasting changes."

"I am grateful for my health and work to maintain it with joy and dedication."

"I let go of unhealthy habits and embrace positive change with an open heart."

"I am worthy of good health, and I actively pursue it every day."

"I am mindful of what I consume, making choices that align with my well-being."

"I embrace challenges as opportunities to grow stronger physically and mentally."

"I surround myself with a supportive community that encourages my healthy choices."

That's it, really, when combined with the simple rituals at the first of this chapter.

CHAPTER SIX

Manifesting Financial Prosperity and Success

By the time you have finished reading this section, you will have gained a comprehensive understanding of the fascinating world of Candle magic, and how it can attract financial prosperity and success into your life. If you are intrigued by witchcraft, the occult, or are simply exploring ways to tap into the power of magik, this section is tailor-made to assist you in manifesting abundance and achieving your financial aspirations.

Candle magik rituals and spells have been used for centuries as a powerful tool for manifesting desires. By harnessing the energy of fire and combining it with intention and visualization, you can create a potent force that aligns with the universe to attract wealth and success.

To begin your journey towards financial prosperity, it is crucial to first examine your beliefs and mindset around money.

Often, subconscious blocks and limiting beliefs can hinder our ability to attract abundance. Through the practice of Candle magik, you can release these negative patterns and replace them with positive affirmations, allowing the flow of wealth and success into your life.

One effective ritual is to choose a green or gold candle, representing financial abundance, and anoint it with a prosperity oil or herb such as cinnamon or basil. As you light the candle, visualize your financial goals and envision yourself already achieving them. Feel the emotions of abundance and success, allowing that energy to radiate from within you.

Incorporating symbols of wealth and prosperity, such as coins or dollar bills, into your ritual can amplify its power. You can place these items around the candle or create a small altar dedicated to financial prosperity. Candle magik rituals are a powerful tool for manifesting your financial goals and desires. Through the practice of visualization and intention, you can create a potent force that will attract wealth and success into your life.

Consistency is key when working with Candle magik for financial success. It is recommended to perform this ritual regularly, perhaps every week or month, to reinforce your intentions and beliefs. By consistently aligning your energy with abundance, you create a powerful magnet for financial opportunities and wealth.

Remember, Candle magik is a tool that works in harmony with the universe, but it also requires action on your part. Take inspired steps towards your financial goals, whether that means seeking new job opportunities, investing wisely, or starting your own business. By combining the power of intention, visualization, and action, you can manifest the financial prosperity and success you desire.

Attracting Opportunities and Abundance into Your Life

The power within candle magic is not only determined by our intentions but also the energy we put forth into the universe. By tapping into the mystical properties of candles, we can open up a world of abundance, full of opportunities and possibilities waiting to be seized. The following section has been specifically designed to assist and lead you on a journey towards attracting various opportunities and abundance into your life.

Whether you are seeking love, healing, prosperity, protection, manifestation, spiritual enlightenment, career success, psychic development, self-love, or lunar and celestial energy, candle magic rituals and spells can be tailored to suit your specific desires. All you need to do it set your intention, choose a candle color, perhaps decide on a mantra, then light the candle and gaze on it while meditating on the mantra you have chosen. To manifest success and opportunities in your life, it is recommended to use a yellow candle. Yellow is a powerful color that is associated with intellect, wisdom, and creativity. As you light the candle, visualize your desired outcome and feel the emotions of success and joy. Imagine yourself already achieving your goals and desires, and allow this positive energy to flow throughout your body.

Besides visualizing success, it is important to take inspired action. Whether you are seeking a new job, a promotion, or a business venture, take steps towards making your dream a reality. This could mean researching potential employers, networking with industry professionals, or reaching out to potential investors. By combining the power of candle magik with inspired action, you can create powerful opportunities and attract abundance into your life.

As part of the ritual, you can also incorporate symbols of abundance, such as coins or dollar bills, into your practice. Place these items around the candle or create a small altar dedicated to manifesting your dreams. This will help to reinforce your intentions and attract positive energy and opportunities into your life.

When it comes to candle magik, consistency is key. It is recommended to perform this ritual regularly, perhaps every week or month, to reinforce your intentions and maintain a positive mindset. Through the practice of visualization, intention, and inspired action, you can manifest the success and abundance you desire.

To attract opportunities and abundance, begin by selecting a candle that resonates with your intention. Green candles are often associated with prosperity and abundance, while gold candles symbolize success and wealth. Light the chosen candle with a focused mind, visualizing the opportunities and abundance you wish to attract.

As the flame dances, recite affirmations or incantations that align with your desires. Speak from a place of certainty and gratitude, believing that the universe is conspiring to bring you the opportunities and abundance you seek.

Consider incorporating additional elements such as crystals, herbs, or oils into your candle magic rituals. Citrine, for example, is known for its ability to attract wealth and abundance, making it an excellent companion to your prosperity rituals. Lavender can promote healing and wellness, while rose quartz can enhance love and relationships.

As you continue to practice candle magic rituals and spells, be open to receiving the opportunities and abundance that come your way. Trust in the process and remain aligned with your intentions. With patience, persistence, and a little magik, you will create a life filled with limitless possibilities.

The path to attract opportunities and abundance is paved with intention, belief, and the willingness to take inspired action. Embrace the power of candle magic, and let the universe guide you towards a life of prosperity and fulfillment.

Removing Blocks to Financial Growth

Even with the power of magik to increase our prosperity and boost income, there are often blocks that hinder our financial growth and prevent us from experiencing the wealth we desire. This section explores various techniques and rituals to remove these obstacles and unlock the path to financial success. One of the most powerful rituals to remove blocks to financial growth is through the use of visualization. This involves seeing yourself as having achieved your goals, and visualizing the abundance that comes with it. Through this practice, you can begin to manifest your financial goals in the physical world.

Another powerful ritual to increase financial success is the use of affirmations. Affirmations are statements that help you focus on your goals and keep your vision of success alive. By repeating these affirmations, you can begin to attract more money and abundance into your life.

Some examples of affirmation in this area are:

I am worthy of success and abundance.

I attract prosperity and financial abundance into my life effortlessly.

I am open to receiving abundance in all forms.

I am a money magnet, and wealth flows to me easily.

I am aligned with the energy of prosperity, and it is manifesting in my life.

I am capable of creating unlimited opportunities for wealth and success.

I am grateful for the abundance that comes into my life daily.

Money comes to me from expected and unexpected sources.

I am constantly discovering new ways to increase my income.

I am confident in my ability to achieve financial freedom.

I am attracting lucrative opportunities that align with my skills and passions.

I am open to receiving money, and I use it wisely to create a positive impact.

I release any limiting beliefs about money and embrace my

abundance mindset.

I am in control of my financial destiny, and I make empowered decisions.

I am deserving of wealth and prosperity, and I allow it to flow into my life.

Finally, it's important to remember that manifesting wealth is a process that requires patience and dedication. Working with the power of magik can help to speed up this process, but it's important to remain consistent in your efforts. With a bit of hard work and determination, you can begin to unlock the path to financial success.

One of the first steps to removing blocks to financial growth is identifying and releasing limiting beliefs surrounding money. Many of us carry deep-rooted beliefs that money is scarce or that we do not deserve wealth. Through candle magik, we can create a ritual to confront and release these beliefs, allowing us to open ourselves to the flow of abundance.

Another powerful technique is the use of intention candles. By selecting a specific candle color and carving symbols or affirmations into the wax, we can focus our intentions on attracting financial prosperity. Lighting these candles during rituals or daily meditations helps to reinforce our desires and align our energy with the vibrations of abundance.

To further enhance our financial growth, it is vital to cleanse and purify our energetic space. Negative energies can create blocks in our path to success. Burning, cleansing candles, and performing rituals to clear away these energies can create a clean slate for financial abundance to enter our lives. Finally, it is important to create an action plan to manifest our financial goals. Once we have identified our beliefs and intentions, it is time to take practical steps to bring our desires into reality. Through dedicated effort and a focus on our goals, we can create the life of abundance that we desire.

Visualization is another potent tool in removing blocks to financial growth. By visualizing ourselves in a state of financial abundance and success, we send a clear message to the universe about our desires. Using visualization techniques during candle magik rituals helps to solidify our intentions and attract the opportunities necessary for financial growth.

Lastly, it is important to remember that financial growth is not solely about material wealth. True abundance encompasses all aspects of our lives, including love, relationships, and overall well-being. Incorporating rituals and spells that focus on these areas alongside our financial rituals can create a holistic approach to prosperity and abundance.

Road Opener/Blocks Removal

A basic Road Opener ritual is as follows;

Using an orange candle, anoint it with a "block buster" oil, available via online outlets or a local new age store. Rub a few drops of this on into the orange candle.

During the Release Cycle, light this candle while focusing on the end result, removal of all blocks.

Allow the candle to burn out, and bury any remaining wax in the ground. Don't worry about leftover wax, or try to read anything special into the patterns caused by the melting wax.

It can't get any simpler than that!

Cultivating a Prosperity Mindset

The connection between candle magic and our ability to manifest our desires is established by our capacity to cultivate a mindset of abundance and prosperity. When we put positive energy into the universe, the abundance that flows into our lives increases directly because of that positivity. I will gently guide you on a transformative journey to unlock the power within and manifest a life of prosperity and abundance.

To begin, it is essential to understand that a prosperity mindset goes beyond mere financial wealth. It encompasses all areas of our lives, including love, relationships, career, wellness, and spiritual enlightenment. By aligning our intentions with the energy of abundance, we can attract positive opportunities and experiences. Honestly, many forget that our mindset maic rituals and spells specifically designed to enhance prosperity and abundance. From simple rituals for attracting financial blessings to spells to open doors of opportunity, you will discover the tools to manifest your desires.

But before diving into the practical aspects, we must delve into the mindset necessary for success. Cultivating a prosperity mindset involves rewiring our thoughts and beliefs, shedding limiting beliefs about money and success. By adopting a positive and abundant mindset, we invite the universe to shower us with blessings.

Throughout this section, we will also explore the connection between prosperity and other areas of our lives, such as love, career, and spiritual growth. By understanding how these aspects intertwine, we can harness their collective power to manifest our desires.

As you progress through the pages of this section, you will find rituals and spells tailored to your specific needs and desires. Whether you seek financial abundance, career success, or a deeper spiritual connection, there is a candle magic ritual or spell waiting to assist you on your journey.

Remember, cultivating a prosperity mindset is an ongoing practice. It requires consistent effort and a commitment to personal growth. By embracing the principles outlined in this section, you will unlock the unlimited potential within you and create a life of abundance and fulfillment.

Get ready to ignite the flame of prosperity within you and watch as the universe aligns to support your every desire. Let the art of candle magic be your guide on this transformative journey to manifesting a life of prosperity and abundance.

Creating a Wealthy and Abundant Future

In this section, we will explore the powerful practice of candle magic and how it can help you manifest prosperity and abundance in your life. Whether you are seeking financial wealth, success in your career, or overall abundance in all areas of your life, candle magic can be a transformative tool.

Candle magic rituals and spells have been used for centuries by those interested in the occult and witchcraft to harness the energy and power of candles to manifest their desires. By infusing intention, visualization, and the energy of the flame, you can align yourself with the vibrations of wealth and abundance.

Love and Relationships Candle Magic Rituals and Spells

Love and relationships are essential aspects of a fulfilled life. In this section, we will explore how candle magic can enhance your love life and attract the ideal partner or deepen the connection with your current partner. By using specific candles and performing rituals with intention, you can ignite the flame of passion and create a loving and harmonious relationship.

Healing and Wellness Candle Magic Rituals and Spells

Health and wellness are vital for a prosperous and abundant future. In this section, we will delve into how candle magic can be used for healing purposes. From physical ailments to emotional wounds, candle magic rituals and spells can aid in your journey towards holistic well-being. By utilizing the energy of candles, you can promote healing and restore balance in your life.

Prosperity and Abundance Candle Magic Rituals and Spells

If you desire financial wealth and abundance, this section is for you. Candle magic can be a powerful tool to attract prosperity and abundance into your life. Through specific rituals and spells, you can align your energy with the frequency of wealth and open yourself up to new opportunities and financial success.

Protection and Cleansing Candle Magic Rituals and Spells

In this section, we will explore how candle magic can assist in protecting yourself and your space from negative energies. By utilizing the power of candles and performing cleansing rituals, you can create a shield of protection around you and clear away any unwanted energies that may hinder your progress towards a wealthy and abundant future.

Manifestation and Law of Attraction Candle Magic Rituals and Spells

The law of attraction is a universal principle that states that like attracts like. In this section, we will explore how candle magic can enhance your ability to manifest your desires. By using candles and performing specific rituals, you can align your thoughts, emotions, and intentions with the energy of abundance and manifest your dreams into reality.

Spiritual Enlightenment and Guidance Candle Magic Rituals and Spells

If you are seeking spiritual enlightenment and guidance on your path towards wealth and abundance, this section is for you. Candle magic can be a transformative tool to connect with higher realms, receive guidance, and gain a deeper understanding of your life's purpose. Through candle magic rituals and spells, you can open yourself up to spiritual insights and align your energy with divine guidance.

Career and Success Candle Magic Rituals and Spells

Whether you are looking to advance in your career or start a new venture, this section will explore how candle magic can enhance your professional success. By utilizing the power of candles and performing specific rituals, you can align yourself with the energy of success, attract new opportunities, and achieve your career goals.

Psychic Development and Intuition Candle Magic Rituals and Spells

Developing your psychic abilities and intuition can greatly enhance your ability to create a wealthy and abundant future. In this section, we will explore how candle magic can aid in psychic development and intuition. Through specific rituals and spells, you can open yourself up to heightened intuition, receive guidance from the spiritual realm, and make more informed decisions on your path towards abundance.

Self-Love and Confidence Candle Magic Rituals and Spells

Self-love and confidence are essential for creating a wealthy and abundant future. In this section, we will explore how candle magic can aid in cultivating self-love and boosting confidence. By utilizing specific candles and performing rituals, you can release self-doubt, embrace your worthiness, and align yourself with the energy of abundance and prosperity.

Lunar and Celestial Energy Candle Magic Rituals and Spells

The moon and celestial energies have long been associated with magic and manifestation. In this section, we will explore how candle magic can harness the power of lunar and celestial energies to enhance your manifestation abilities. By aligning your rituals with specific moon phases and celestial events, you can amplify the energy of your candle magic and manifest your desires more effectively.

In conclusion, candle magic rituals and spells can be a transformative tool for creating a wealthy and abundant future. By exploring the various niches of candle magic, such as love and relationships, healing and wellness, prosperity and abundance, protection and cleansing, manifestation and law of attraction, spiritual enlightenment and guidance, career and success, psychic development and intuition, self-love and confidence, and lunar and celestial energy, you can unlock the power within and manifest your dreams into reality.

7-Day Money Bring

As the title says, this is a 7-day ritual.

You will require 7 green candles, ideally the small 18-hr votive, or the 7-day glass votive. You will need a safe spot to burn these candles and each candle needs to be burned completely.

A single red candle, a straight taper type, or chime candle, prepared as a reversing candle.

A yellow candle to activate lines of communication to help allow money to flow to you.

This ritual begins the day of the Bring Cycle.

Day 1 - light red reversed candle.

While the red burns down, light a green candle

Day 2 through Day 7, start a new candle each day.

(You will wind up with as many as three 7-day candles going at once)

After Day 4, add the yellow candle, but just for one day.

(If you have a case lot of green candles, you may elect to continue burning candles until all are used. However, never start a candle that will not finish burning by the time the Bing Cycle ends.)

CHAPTER SEVEN

Warding off Negative Energies and Entities

When practicing candle magik, it is crucial to not only focus on harnessing positive energies but also take measures to shield oneself from negative energies and entities that might interfere with the desired outcome. Negative energies can manifest in various forms, such as unexplained fatigue, a feeling of heaviness, or an overall sense of unease. These energies can disrupt one's well-being and hinder the effectiveness of magikal rituals and spells. Therefore, it is crucial to learn how to ward off and cleanse oneself and the environment from these negative influences.

Magik tends to make you more aware of the negative energies in the world around you. As you become more aware, these energies can actually attach to you, like sticky mud, to the bottom of your shoe. To protect yourself from these energies, it is important to first be aware of them and then create an energy shield around yourself. This can be done by visualizing a white light surrounding your body that repels negative energies. You might also suddenly come to the attention of people with a general nasty disposition. Their nasty energy can attach to you as well. To protect yourself from these people, it is important to set boundaries and be assertive about what you will and will not accept from people.

Besides protecting yourself from negative energies, it is also important to cleanse and purify the environment before performing any magikal rituals and spells. Smudging is a great way to cleanse the space of any negative energies and to prepare the environment for your spell. Smudging can be done with various herbs, such as sage, cedar, or sweetgrass. You can also use crystals to purify the space by placing them in the four corners of the room or around the ritual area.

My favorite way of clearing a space is using Frankincense resin in a burner. I will move from room to room in my house, spreading the purifying smoke from the incense. Frankincense has been used since the beginning of time to purify spaces like temples and churches. So it'll work in your home. The most important thing to remember when warding off negative energies or entities is to stay positive and trust in the universe. Negative energies and entities are attracted to fear and doubt, so it is important to stay confident and positive in your magikal practice.

Finally, it is important to be mindful of any entities that might be attracted to your magikal practice. These entities can be benevolent or malevolent and can interfere with the outcome of your spell. To protect yourself from these entities, it is important to call upon your spirit guides and ask them to help protect you and your ritual space. You can also set the intention to only invite positive energies into your space. It is also important to remain aware of your energy and to keep it balanced throughout the ritual.

By taking simple steps to protect and purify your space, you can ensure that your magikal ritual and spells are successful and your energy remains clear and balanced.

Another way to ward off negative energies is to use protective magikal symbols and sigils. These symbols can be drawn or inscribed in the air, on objects, and even on your body. They can create an energy field of protection and help to keep out any negative entities that may be present.

Finally, cleansing rituals can remove negative energies and entities from yourself and your environment. These rituals can involve the use of herbs, incense, crystals, and other magikal tools to clear away any unwanted energies. By cleansing yourself and your environment regularly, you can help to protect yourself from any negative influences that may be present.

One way to ward off negative energies is through the use of protection candles. These candles are specially crafted and charged to create a shield of positive energy around the individual or space. When lighting a protection candle, envision a white, impenetrable bubble surrounding you, repelling any negativity that tries to enter your space. You can enhance the candle's energy by anointing it with protective oils, such as frankincense or myrrh, and surrounding it with protective crystals like black tourmaline or obsidian.

Another method to ward off negative energies is by performing a cleansing ritual. This ritual can involve smudging with sage or palo santo, which helps to purify the surrounding energy. Start by lighting the smudge stick and waving it around your body, paying attention to areas that feel heavy or stagnant. As the smoke rises, visualize it absorbing and transmuting any negativity into positive energy. You can also incorporate cleansing herbs, such as rosemary or lavender, into your ritual baths or as incense to further cleanse your energy.

Creating a protective talisman is another powerful technique to ward off negative energies. This can be done by selecting a crystal or charm that resonates with your intention, such as black obsidian for protection or a pentagram for spiritual defense. Hold the talisman in your hands and infuse it with your intention, stating affirmations like "I am shielded from all negative energies and entities." Carry the talisman with you or place it in a prominent location in your home to serve as a constant reminder of your protection.

Remember, the key to warding off negative energies and entities is to maintain a strong and positive energy field. Regularly cleanse yourself and your space, and stay mindful of the people and environments you surround yourself with. By incorporating these practices into your candle magik rituals and spells, you can ensure that you are working from a place of strength and protection, allowing your intentions to manifest in their highest form.

Creating a Safe and Protected Space

Before you begin spell-casting and performing rituals in the captivating realm of candle magic, it is crucial to create a secure and protected environment. By devoting special attention to creating a sacred environment that nurtures and safeguards your energy, you can experience the full transformative power of candle magik, as this section will explore in depth.

When practicing candle magik, it is crucial to remember that you are working with energy, both within yourself and in the universe. Therefore, establishing a safe space ensures that you are shielded from any negative influences or unwanted energies that may interfere with the effectiveness of your spells and rituals.

To begin, cleanse your space using a purifying technique that resonates with you. This could involve smudging with sage, sprinkling salt, or using essential oils to clear any stagnant or negative energy. As you cleanse, visualize a protective shield encompassing your space, warding off any external disturbances.

Next, create an altar or sacred space dedicated solely to your candle magik practice. This area should reflect your intentions and desires, acting as a focal point for your energy and intentions. Place objects that hold personal significance, such as crystals, symbols, or photographs, to enhance the energy and connection to your desired outcomes.

Ensure that your altar is adorned with candles that resonate with your specific intention or desire. For example, if you are seeking love and relationships, use pink or red candles. If you are focused on healing and wellness, opt for green or blue candles. Each candle color holds its own unique energy and vibration, amplifying the potency of your rituals and spells.

As you ignite your candles, invoke the elements and call upon the divine energies that resonate with your intention. This could involve reciting incantations, prayers, or affirmations that align with your desired outcome. Feel the energy of the universe flowing through you, empowering your spells and rituals.

Throughout your candle magik practice, it is essential to maintain a strong energetic boundary. Visualize a protective shield surrounding you, deflecting any negative or unwanted energies. This shield acts as a barrier, ensuring that you remain in a safe and protected space, free from external interference.

By creating a safe and protected space, you empower yourself to fully embrace the transformative power of candle magik. Your spells and rituals will be enhanced, and your intentions will manifest with greater clarity and speed. Embrace the power within and let your candle magik journey unfold in a space that is nurtured and safeguarded.

Banishing and Cleansing Rituals

In the realm of candle magic, banishing and cleansing rituals hold significant importance. These rituals are essential for clearing negative energy, removing obstacles, and creating a harmonious environment. Whether you are seeking protection, releasing past traumas, or banishing unwanted influences, these powerful rituals can guide you on your path to spiritual enlightenment and empowerment.

Banishing rituals are designed to rid ourselves of negative energies, toxic relationships, or unhealthy patterns. By harnessing the power of intention and the energy of candles, we can cleanse our space and our minds, creating a fresh start. To perform a banishing ritual, set up a sacred space, light a black candle, and visualize the negative energy dissolving away. As the candle burns, repeat affirmations or incantations that resonate with your goals, such as "I release all that no longer serves me" or "I banish negativity from my life."

Cleansing rituals focus on purifying our energy and the surrounding space. These rituals are useful after a period of emotional turmoil, illness, or when moving into a new home. By incorporating candles into your cleansing rituals, you can amplify the energy and create a sacred atmosphere. Begin by lighting a white candle, symbolizing purity and clarity. As the flame flickers, imagine its light purifying your energy field and the surrounding space. You may choose to use herbs, crystals, or essential oils that resonate with cleansing properties, such as sage, lavender, or rosemary.

It is important to note that banishing and cleansing rituals should be performed with respect and reverence. Before embarking on any magical practice, take the time to ground yourself, center your energy, and set clear intentions. Remember to always practice within your own belief system and honor the traditions that resonate with you.

In the following chapters, we will explore specific candle magic rituals for banishing and cleansing in various areas of life. Whether you seek to banish negative influences in love and relationships, attract prosperity and abundance, or enhance your psychic abilities, the power of candle magic can assist you on your journey. By harnessing the energy of candles and combining it with intention, visualization, and ritual, you can unlock the power within and manifest your desires.

Shielding and Psychic Protection

When it comes to the realm of witchcraft and the occult, it is absolutely vital to comprehend the significance of shielding and psychic protection. It is important to acknowledge that protecting our energetic selves from negative influences and psychic attacks is just as vital as safeguarding our physical bodies. By reading through this section, you will gain an understanding of the various methods and practices used to shield oneself from negative energies and psychic attacks, which will equip you with the tools to strengthen and protect your spiritual wellbeing.

Shielding is the practice of creating a protective barrier around yourself or your space, preventing unwanted energies from infiltrating your aura. Psychic protection, on the other hand, involves strengthening your energetic boundaries and warding off negative entities or influences. Together, these practices offer a shield against harmful energies that can drain your vitality and impede your magical endeavors.

One powerful method of shielding is through the use of candle magic. By incorporating specific candles and intentions, you can create a shield that acts as a barrier against negativity. This section delves into various candle magic rituals and spells tailored to shielding and psychic protection. From visualization techniques to the use of protective herbs and crystals, you will learn how to craft an impenetrable shield of energy.

To enhance your psychic protection, this section offers a range of rituals and spells that harness the power of candle magic. Whether you seek to banish negative energies or build a psychic shield, these rituals can be tailored to suit your specific needs. From invoking angelic or elemental energies to setting up protective altars, you will discover how to fortify your psychic defenses.

Besides creating a shield, it is important to regularly reinforce and maintain it. This section delves into the various techniques for amplifying and strengthening your protective barriers. From cleansing and purifying rituals to the use of sigils and affirmations, you will learn how to keep your shield intact and continuously strong.

Shielding and psychic protection are integral aspects of the magical arts. By incorporating candle magic rituals and spells, you can enhance your ability to ward off negativity and cultivate a safe and harmonious, energetic space. Whether you are seeking protection from external influences, psychic attacks, or simply wish to fortify your spiritual wellbeing, the techniques explored in this section will empower you to unlock the power within and embrace a life filled with positive energy and spiritual enlightenment.

Purifying and Cleansing Personal Energy

The power and effectiveness of candle magic is not solely dependent on the flickering flame, but also on the energy that we infuse into the practice. The ability of candles to cleanse and purify spaces is well known, but what many people don't realize is that they can also purify and cleanse our personal energy.

Our personal energy is the essence of who we are. It can be influenced by various factors, such as stress, negativity, or even the energy of others. When our personal energy becomes stagnant or imbalanced, it can hinder our ability to manifest our desires and attract positive outcomes.

To begin the process of purifying and cleansing personal energy, it is essential to create a sacred space. This space should be free from distractions and filled with positive energy. Light a white candle, symbolizing purity and clarity, and focus on its flame as you set your intention to cleanse and purify your energy.

One powerful technique for purifying personal energy is visualization. Close your eyes and imagine a bright, golden light surrounding your body. See this light expanding and enveloping you, washing away any negative or stagnant energy. As you visualize, imagine yourself becoming lighter and more vibrant with each breath.

Another effective method is the use of cleansing herbs and oils. Sage, lavender, and frankincense are all known for their purifying properties. Create a cleansing blend by combining these herbs or oils and anointing your candle with this mixture before lighting it. As the candle burns, visualize the smoke carrying away any impurities from your energy field.

You can also incorporate crystals into your purification ritual. Clear quartz, amethyst, and selenite are effective for cleansing and purifying energy. Hold the crystal in your hand and set the intention for it to absorb any negativity or impurities. Place the crystal next to the candle as it burns, allowing its energy to infuse with the cleansing flame.

Remember, the key to purifying and cleansing personal energy is consistency and intention. Make it a regular practice to cleanse your energy field, especially after challenging experiences or encounters with negative energy. By doing so, you will create a clear and vibrant, energetic space that allows for the manifestation of your desires and the attraction of positive energy into your life.

CHAPTER EIGHT

Harnessing the Power of Intention and Manifestation

I have a book on using High Magik to leverage the Law of Attraction, using gods and daemons. The Law of Attraction gets a much-needed boost in that manner. The same effect is seen when combining candles and the Law of Attraction. The candles represent the energy of the gods and daemons and the Law of Attraction is used to draw the desired outcome. The combination of the two is incredibly powerful and can manifest whatever you desire.

Using candle magik, the power of intention and manifestation holds tremendous potential for those who seek to unlock the hidden forces within. This chapter, we're going to peek at the effects of harnessing this power to create positive change in various aspects of life, catering to the diverse interests of our readers. The first step is to make sure your intentions are clear.

When setting your intentions, you want to focus on the result that you would like to achieve, not just the means to get there. Focus on how you want to feel after the desired outcome has been achieved. Make sure to maintain a positive attitude and a clear vision of what you want to achieve.

The next step is to set up your environment to support your intention. This could include setting up a ritual altar, lighting candles and incense, or playing calming music. This will help you stay focused and generate the energy needed to manifest your desired outcome.

Once your environment is set up, the next step is to enter a meditative state. This is important, as it allows you to reach a deeper level of connection with your intention. In this state of awareness, you become more connected to your subconscious mind, opening the door to the channels of the Universe that will help you manifest your desired outcome.

The next step is to use visualization to create a mental image of the outcome you desire. Visualization is an incredibly powerful tool that can help you cre us on a journey to financial and material success. By aligning our intentions with the energy of abundance, we can attract prosperity, increase our wealth, and create a life of abundance and fulfillment.

Protection and Cleansing Candle Magic Rituals and Spells offer a shield against negative energies and a means to purify our surroundings. By harnessing the power of candles, we can safeguard ourselves, our homes, and our loved ones, creating a safe and sacred space to thrive.

Manifestation and Law of Attraction Candle Magic Rituals and Spells dive into the art of manifesting our desires. By focusing our intention and utilizing the law of attraction, we can manifest our dreams into reality, bringing forth the life we envision.

Spiritual Enlightenment and Guidance Candle Magic Rituals and Spells provide a pathway to inner wisdom and divine connection. By tapping into the spiritual energy of candles, we can deepen our understanding of the universe, receive guidance from higher realms, and expand our spiritual horizons.

Career and Success Candle Magic Rituals and Spells illuminate the path to professional achievement. By harnessing the power of intention, we can attract opportunities, enhance our skills, and manifest success in our chosen endeavors.

Psychic Development and Intuition Candle Magic Rituals and Spells offer a gateway to unlocking our innate psychic abilities. By working with candles, we can enhance our intuition, develop clairvoyance, and strengthen our connection to the spiritual realm.

Self-Love and Confidence Candle Magic Rituals and Spells empower us to embrace our true selves. By infusing candles with self-love and confidence, we can overcome self-doubt, cultivate a positive self-image, and embrace our unique beauty.

Lunar and Celestial Energy Candle Magic Rituals and Spells tap into the mystical powers of the moon and the celestial realms. By aligning our intentions with the lunar cycle and harnessing the energy of the cosmos, we can amplify the potency of our rituals and spells, inviting divine energy into our lives.

Within the pages of this chapter, you will find a treasure trove of knowledge, rituals, and spells tailored to your specific interests. By harnessing the power of intention and manifestation through candle magik, you have the ability to unlock the power within and create a life of magic, fulfillment, and transformation.

Aligning with the Law of Attraction

The Law of Attraction, which is a fundamental principle, holds immense power and has the ability to transform lives. The universal law of attraction operates on the belief that similar things tend to attract one another, and by tapping into this principle, we can bring to fruition our most profound aspirations and effectuate a metamorphosis in our existence. In this particular section, we will delve deeper into the intrinsic relationship that exists between the Law of Attraction and the practice of candle magic, thereby providing you with the necessary tools to connect with this potent force and bring your desires into fruition.

Candle magic rituals and spells provide a tangible and visually captivating way to focus your intentions and communicate with the universe. By lighting a candle and infusing it with your desires, you are creating a channel of energy that amplifies your intentions and sends them out into the universe.

When performing candle magic rituals and spells, it is essential to align yourself with the Law of Attraction. This means cultivating a positive mindset, believing wholeheartedly in the power of your intentions, and releasing any doubts or fears that may hinder your manifestation process. Remember, the universe responds to the energy you emit, so maintaining a high vibrational state is crucial.

To align with the Law of Attraction, begin by clarifying your intentions and visualizing them with absolute clarity. As you light your candle, imagine your desires coming to life, feeling the emotions associated with their manifestation. Hold onto this vision throughout your ritual, allowing the candle's flame to serve as a beacon, attracting your desires towards you.

Incorporating affirmations and positive statements into your candle magic rituals can further enhance your alignment with the Law of Attraction. Repeat empowering phrases that reinforce your belief in the manifestation of your desires. By affirming your intentions, you are strengthening your connection with the universe and solidifying your alignment with the Law of Attraction.

It is important to remember that the Law of Attraction requires patience and trust. It may take time for your desires to manifest, but by consistently aligning yourself with the energy of the universe and maintaining a positive mindset, you are creating the ideal conditions for your intentions to come to fruition.

As you delve deeper into the world of candle magic and explore its various niches, such as love and relationships, healing and wellness, prosperity and abundance, protection and cleansing, manifestation and the Law of Attraction, spiritual enlightenment and guidance, career and success, psychic development and intuition, self-love and confidence, and lunar and celestial energy, remember that aligning with the Law of Attraction is the key to unlocking the immense power within. Embrace this universal law, infuse your rituals with intention and positivity, and watch as your desires manifest before your very eyes.

Manifesting Specific Desires and Goals

Through the focused energy and intention that you channel into your candle rituals, you can unlock the unlimited potential of the universe to bring forth what you truly desire. Whether you seek love, healing, prosperity, protection, or guidance, candle magik can be your trusted ally on this transformative journey.

If you yearn for deep, meaningful love or wish to strengthen an existing relationship, candle magik can help you attract and nurture the bonds of love. By selecting the right candles, anointing them with oils, and performing rituals with intention and love, you can invite the energy of love into your life and keep it burning brightly.

Candle magik offers a powerful tool for promoting physical, emotional, and spiritual healing. By focusing the energy of specific candles, herbs, and crystals, you can release negative energy, alleviate pain, and restore balance within yourself or others. Whether you seek relief from a physical ailment or wish to heal a broken heart, candle magik rituals can support your journey towards holistic wellness.

If you desire financial stability, success, and abundance, candle magik can help you align with the energy of prosperity. By utilizing candles of the appropriate color, incorporating abundance-affirming herbs and symbols, and performing rituals with gratitude and belief, you can attract the wealth and opportunities you seek into your life.

In a world filled with negative energies and unwanted influences, candle magik rituals can provide you with a shield of protection and a sense of inner peace. By harnessing the power of specific candles, herbs, and crystals, you can create a sacred space, banish negative energies, and cleanse your aura. Whether you seek protection from psychic attacks or wish to purify your living environment, candle magik can be your trusted ally.

The law of attraction states that like attracts like, and through candle magik, you can harness this universal law to manifest your desires. By visualizing your goals, selecting the appropriate candles, and performing rituals infused with intention and belief, you can align with the energy of manifestation and attract your dreams into reality.

For those seeking spiritual growth, guidance, and enlightenment, candle magik rituals can serve as a sacred pathway to higher consciousness. By incorporating candles, oils, and crystals that resonate with your spiritual journey, you can connect with divine energies, receive guidance from your spirit guides, and deepen your connection with the universe.

Whether you are seeking a new job, a promotion, or success in your current career, candle magik rituals can help you manifest your professional goals. By selecting candles that align with your intentions and incorporating corresponding herbs and symbols, you can infuse your rituals with the energy of success, confidence, and abundance.

Candle magik can also be a powerful tool for enhancing your psychic abilities and intuition. By selecting candles that resonate with psychic energy, incorporating divination tools, and performing rituals with focus and intention, you can awaken and strengthen your psychic gifts, allowing you to tap into the hidden realms of wisdom and insight.

To cultivate self-love, boost confidence, and embrace your true potential, candle magik rituals can be a transformative practice. By selecting candles that symbolize self-love and empowerment, anointing them with oils, and performing rituals with the intention of embracing your worth, you can heal past wounds, release self-doubt, and step into your authentic power.

By harnessing the energy of the moon and celestial bodies, candle magik rituals can amplify your intentions and manifestations. By performing rituals during specific lunar phases, selecting candles that align with the moon's energy, and incorporating celestial correspondences, you can tap into the cosmic forces that govern the universe and co-create your reality.

Enhancing Visualization and Affirmation Techniques

Visualization and affirmation techniques are powerful tools that can greatly enhance the effectiveness of your candle magic rituals and spells. By incorporating these techniques into your practice, you can strengthen your intentions, focus your energy, and manifest your desires more effectively.

Visualizing your desires is a crucial step in candle magic. When you light a candle, take a moment to close your eyes and imagine your goal as vividly as possible. See yourself already in possession of what you desire. Imagine the details, the feelings, and the emotions associated with achieving your goal. By visualizing your desires, you are creating a clear mental image that the universe can work with.

To enhance your visualization, you can also create a vision board or a manifestation journal. Collect images, quotes, and affirmations that represent your desires and create a visual representation of your goals. Place this vision board or journal in a prominent place where you can see it daily. By regularly looking at your vision board or reading your manifestation journal, you reinforce your intentions and keep them at the forefront of your mind.

Affirmations are positive statements that affirm your desires as already being true. By repeating affirmations during your candle magic rituals, you are programming your subconscious mind to believe in the reality of your desires. Choose affirmations that resonate with your goals and state them with conviction. For example, if you are performing a love and relationships candle magic ritual, you could repeat affirmations such as "I am worthy of a loving and fulfilling relationship" or "Love flows to me effortlessly and abundantly."

To enhance the effectiveness of your affirmations, combine them with the power of candle magic. As you light your candle, state your affirmations out loud, visualizing your desires as you speak. Feel the energy of the candle amplifying your intentions and affirmations, and believe in their manifestation.

Remember, consistency and belief are key when using visualization and affirmation techniques in your candle magic practice. Continuously visualize your desires, repeat your affirmations, and trust in the power of your intentions. As you develop your skills in visualization and affirmation, you will witness the incredible potential of candle magic to transform your life in all areas, from love and relationships to prosperity and abundance, and beyond.

Optimizing Your Manifestation Practice

Manifestation is the art of bringing your desires into physical reality through focused intention and energy. It is a powerful tool that can be enhanced and optimized through various techniques. In this section, we will explore ways to optimize your manifestation practice and increase your success rate in achieving your goals.

1. Clarify your intentions: Before starting any manifestation ritual or spell, it is essential to have a clear understanding of what you truly desire. Take the time to reflect and write down your intentions in specific and detailed terms. This clarity will help you align your energy and focus towards your desired outcome.

2. Create a sacred space: Designate a specific area in your home as your sacred space for manifestation rituals. Cleanse and purify the space using cleansing herbs or incense. Decorate it with

candles, crystals, and meaningful objects that resonate with your intentions. This sacred space will serve as a physical representation of your intentions and amplify the energy you generate during your rituals.

3. Harness the power of visualization: Visualization is a powerful tool in manifestation. Close your eyes and visualize yourself already living your desired reality. Engage all your senses and feel the emotions associated with achieving your goals. The more vivid and detailed your visualization, the stronger the energetic imprint you create.

4. Use affirmations and mantras: Affirmations and mantras are powerful tools to reprogram your subconscious mind and shift your beliefs towards manifestation. Choose affirmations that resonate with your desires and repeat them daily. Write them down on small pieces of paper and place them near your candles during rituals.

5. Align with the moon phases: The moon exerts a strong influence on our energy and emotions. By aligning your manifestation rituals with the different moon phases, you can harness the lunar energy to amplify your intentions. New moon rituals are ideal for setting new intentions, while full moon rituals are perfect for releasing and letting go of what no longer serves you.

6. Practice gratitude and detachment: Cultivating an attitude of gratitude and detachment is essential in the manifestation process. Express gratitude for what you already have and trust that the universe will provide for your needs. Detach from the outcome

and surrender the timing and details to the divine forces at work. This aspect is often overlooked by students of the occult. You seriously have to detach from the results to have them manifest. It sounds quite odd, but by focusing on the outcome, and wondering WHEN, it'll just delay the manifestation. Let go of the results, and trust in the power of intention.

7. Honor the divine: Lastly, honor and give thanks to the divine forces that are helping you manifest your desires. Ask the gods and goddesses for their assistance in your manifestation journey. Offer your gratitude and thanks for all that you have received and all that is yet to come.

By implementing these optimization techniques into your manifestation practice, you can enhance your ability to manifest your desires. Remember that patience, persistence, and faith are key ingredients. Trust in your own power and the universal energies that support you, and watch as your dreams become a tangible reality.

CHAPTER NINE

Connecting with Spirit Guides and Higher Self

I love connecting with guides. All while growing up, I kept hearing about these spirits guides, and the entire concept came into focus in 1984, when I read that an author of the Death and Dying books was meditating and connecting to her guides, I needed to do this as well. And yet, despite my eagerness to do this, it remained elusive. It seemed the harder I tried, the harder it got.

Finally, after years of practice, I began to make more consistent progress in connecting with my guides. I started to learn how to tune in and ask for their guidance. I learned to listen to my inner voice and trust that the guidance I received was true and authentic. I also learned to connect with my Higher Self, which is the highest part of myself that knows all truth and wisdom.

When I first started connecting with my Spirit Guides, I was unsurprised to find out how much love and guidance they offered.

I am so grateful for the connection and the wisdom they have shared with me. I believe it has made a huge difference in my life and I am deeply grateful for the support and guidance I have received.

Connecting with my Spirit Guides and Higher Self has been a powerful and transformational experience for me. I have found that when I am connected; I feel joy, peace, and clarity. I am able to make better decisions and gain a deeper understanding of life. I also have a greater sense of purpose and direction. I feel more empowered and connected to the divine.

It's an incredible feeling to know that I have access to this higher knowing and guidance. I am so grateful for these experiences and the wisdom I have gained from them.

When it comes to the world of candle magik, nothing is quite as transformative as connecting with our spirit guides and higher self. When we embark on our journey, we can count on the presence of these spiritual allies who assist us. Their valuable insight and support are what we need to navigate through life's complexities, and luckily, they are always willing to share it with us. The energy that we can draw from others is a powerful tool, allowing us to reveal our hidden potential and effortlessly bring our desires to fruition.

To begin this sacred practice, it is essential to create a space that is conducive to spiritual connection. Find a quiet and comfortable area where you can be alone with your thoughts. Light a candle, preferably one that aligns with your intention, and allow its gentle flame to guide you into a state of relaxation and receptivity.

Once you are centered, take a moment to set your intention for the connection. Clearly state your desire to connect with your spirit guides and higher self, asking for their guidance and wisdom. Visualize a bright light surrounding you, protecting and guiding you throughout this spiritual journey.

Now, it is time to open the lines of communication. There are various techniques you can use to connect with your spirit guides and higher self, such as meditation, automatic writing, or simply speaking aloud. Choose the method that resonates with you and feels most natural.

During this process, it is important to remain open and receptive to the messages and insights that come through. Trust your intuition and allow your spirit guides and higher self to speak directly to your heart and mind. Be patient, as it may take time to establish a clear and consistent connection.

As you deepen your relationship with your spirit guides and higher self, you will discover a wealth of knowledge and wisdom within yourself. They will offer guidance on various aspects of your life, whether it be love and relationships, healing and wellness, prosperity and abundance, or protection and cleansing. They can also assist you in manifesting your desires, finding spiritual enlightenment and guidance, achieving career success, developing your psychic abilities, cultivating self-love and confidence, and harnessing the energy of the lunar and celestial realms.

Remember, the key to connecting with your spirit guides and

higher self is to approach this practice with an open heart and mind. Trust in the process and believe in the power within. As you cultivate this sacred connection, you will uncover a world of infinite possibilities and tap into the true essence of your being. Embrace the magik that lies within you and let your spirit guides and higher self be your guiding light on this transformative journey.

Seeking Divine Wisdom and Guidance

We can use candle magik to help us connect with the divine within us and the divine forces around us. By setting up a meditation space, and working with candles, you can focus and meditate on connecting with your guides and higher self.

Timing for this is independent of the Moon cycles. So don't worry about if it's the "Bring" or the "Release" cycle while working in this chapter.

In order to embark on this spiritual journey, it is essential to create a sacred space that facilitates a deep connection with the divine. Begin by selecting a candle that resonates with your intention and the specific energy you wish to invoke. For seeking divine wisdom and guidance, a white or purple candle is often ideal, as these colors are associated with spirituality and higher consciousness.

Before lighting the candle, take a moment to center yourself and enter a state of mindfulness. Close your eyes and focus on your breath, allowing any distractions to melt away. Once you feel centered, visualize a beam of white light emanating from the candle, reaching up towards the heavens. Imagine this light connecting you to the divine source of wisdom and guidance.

As the candle burns, use this time to meditate and pose your questions to the universe. Be open and receptive to the insights and messages that come to you. Pay attention to any synchronicities, signs, or symbols that may appear in your daily life, as they may hold significant meaning and guidance.

To enhance your connection with the divine, you may choose to incorporate specific herbs, crystals, or essential oils that are known for their spiritual properties. For example, burning sage or lavender can purify the space and promote a sense of clarity and receptivity. Amethyst or clear quartz crystals can amplify your intentions and aid in receiving divine insights.

Remember, seeking divine wisdom and guidance is an ongoing practice. It is not a onetime event, but rather a lifelong journey of growth and discovery. Each time you engage in candle magik with the intention of connecting with the divine, you deepen your spiritual connection and expand your consciousness.

By incorporating this ritual into your candle magik practice, you invite the wisdom of the divine into your life, empowering you to make enlightened decisions and navigate your path with clarity and purpose. Embrace this opportunity to seek divine guidance and watch as your spiritual journey unfolds before you, illuminating the way towards your highest potential.

Expanding Consciousness and Spiritual Growth

In the realm of candle magic, there lies a transformative power that can unlock your true potential and guide you on a path of spiritual growth. Through the art of candle magic, you can expand your consciousness and connect with the divine forces that reside within and around you. This section delves into the profound effects that candle magic rituals and spells have on various aspects of your life, including love and relationships, healing and wellness, prosperity and abundance, protection and cleansing, manifestation and law of attraction, spiritual enlightenment and guidance, career and success, psychic development and intuition, self-love and confidence, as well as lunar and celestial energy.

Candle magic rituals and spells related to love and relationships can help you attract a soul-mate, enhance intimacy, and heal old wounds. By harnessing the energy of specific candles and incorporating intention and visualization, you can create a powerful ritual that brings love and harmony into your life.

For those seeking healing and wellness, candle magic rituals and spells can be utilized to promote physical and emotional well-being. By selecting candles associated with healing properties and incorporating affirmations and energy healing techniques, you can tap into the transformative energy of candle magic to support your healing journey.

The pursuit of prosperity and abundance is another area where candle magic can play a significant role. By aligning your intentions with the energy of abundance and using candles that symbolize wealth and success, you can manifest financial prosperity and create a life of abundance.

Protection and cleansing are crucial aspects of spiritual growth, and candle magic rituals and spells can provide a shield of energetic protection while purifying your space and aura. Utilizing specific candles and incorporating rituals to ward off negative energies and cleanse your environment can create a safe and sacred space for spiritual exploration and growth.

Manifestation and the law of attraction are powerful tools for creating the life you desire. By using candles to amplify your intentions and focusing your energy on your desired outcomes, you can harness the power of the universe to manifest your dreams and goals.

This section also explores candle magic rituals and spells for spiritual enlightenment and guidance, career and success, psychic development and intuition, self-love and confidence, as well as lunar and celestial energy. Each section provides guidance, techniques, and rituals tailored to these specific areas of interest, allowing you to delve deeper into your spiritual journey and unlock the hidden potentials within.

Think of the art of candle magic as a gateway to expanding consciousness and achieving spiritual growth. By incorporating these rituals and spells into your life, you can tap into the ancient wisdom and power of candle magic to manifest your desires, heal your wounds, and connect with the divine forces that surround you. Embark on this transformative journey and unlock the power within through the art of candle magic.

Deepening Meditation and Mindfulness Practices

In the realm of candle magic, it is essential to cultivate a deep connection with oneself and the energies surrounding us. One way to enhance this connection is through the practice of deepening meditation and mindfulness. By incorporating these practices into your candle magic rituals and spells, you can unlock the full potential of your intentions and manifest your desires more effectively.

Meditation is a powerful tool that allows us to quiet the mind, focus our energy, and tap into our subconscious mind. Through regular meditation, we can develop a heightened sense of awareness and increase our ability to channel and direct energy. This is particularly beneficial for individuals interested in witchcraft, the occult, and magic, as it strengthens the connection to the spiritual realm and enhances our intuitive abilities.

When it comes to candle magic rituals and spells, incorporating mindfulness is essential. Mindfulness is the act of being fully present in the moment, observing and acknowledging our thoughts and emotions without judgment. By practicing mindfulness during your candle magic rituals, you can bring a deeper level of intention and awareness to your spell work. This allows you to align your thoughts, emotions, and actions with your desired outcome, increasing the potency of your magic.

To deepen your meditation and mindfulness practices, consider incorporating techniques such as breath work, visualization, and mantra repetition. These techniques help calm the mind, center your energy, and create a sacred space for your candle magic rituals. Additionally, incorporating grounding exercises and setting clear intentions before each session can further enhance your connection to the energies at play.

Remember, the key to deepening your meditation and mindfulness practices lies in consistency and dedication. Set aside a specific time each day to engage in these practices, even if it's just a few minutes. Over time, you will notice a significant improvement in your ability to focus, channel energy, and manifest your desires through candle magic.

Whether you are seeking love and relationships, healing and wellness, prosperity and abundance, protection and cleansing, or any other specific intention, deepening your meditation and mindfulness practices will amplify the effects of your candle magic rituals and spells. By cultivating a strong connection with yourself and the surrounding energies, you can unlock the true power within and manifest your desires with greater ease and precision. Embrace the transformative potential of deepening meditation and mindfulness, and watch as your candle magic practice reaches new heights of success and fulfillment.

Opening the Third Eye and Developing Psychic Abilities

In the mystical realm of witchcraft and the occult, the concept of opening the third eye and developing psychic abilities holds a significant place. It is a gateway to unlocking the vast potential within oneself and connecting with the unseen energies that surround us. This section delves into the secrets and techniques of accessing this profound power and developing psychic abilities through the art of candle magik.

Candle magik rituals and spells have long been revered for their ability to enhance psychic awareness and intuition. By combining the symbolic power of candles with focused intention and visualization, practitioners can tap into their innate psychic abilities and strengthen their connection with the spiritual realm.

Love and Relationships Candle Magic Rituals and Spells, Healing and Wellness Candle Magic Rituals and Spells, Prosperity and Abundance Candle Magic Rituals and Spells, and various other niches of candle magik provide a solid foundation for psychic development. These rituals and spells not only serve specific purposes but also act as catalysts for unlocking the third eye and expanding one's psychic potential.

Within these rituals, practitioners are guided to create sacred spaces, cleanse their energy, and engage in meditation and visualization techniques. Through these practices, the mind becomes attuned to higher frequencies, allowing the third eye to open and psychic abilities to flourish.

The journey towards psychic development is not merely about acquiring supernatural abilities, but also about seeking spiritual enlightenment and guidance. Candle magik rituals and spells designed to connect with celestial and lunar energies play a vital role in this aspect. These rituals enable practitioners to align themselves with the cosmic forces and receive divine guidance, which further enhances their psychic abilities.

As one delves deeper into the mystical realm of witchcraft and the occult, they will discover the immense power that lies within their own being. By unlocking the third eye and developing psychic abilities, individuals can embark on a transformative journey that brings them closer to self-love, confidence, and success. Moreover, the heightened intuition and psychic awareness gained through these practices can be applied to various aspects of life, including love, relationships, healing, wellness, and career.

In conclusion, opening the third eye and developing psychic abilities through the art of candle magik is a profound and transformative practice. It is a gateway to spiritual enlightenment, divine guidance, and a deeper understanding of oneself and the universe. By incorporating these rituals and spells into their practice, individuals interested in witchcraft, the occult, and magik can embark on a journey of self-discovery and unlock their true potential.

CHAPTER TEN

Attracting Job Opportunities and Career Advancement

In the realm of candle magik, the power to manifest your desires extends far beyond love and relationships, healing and wellness, prosperity and abundance, protection and cleansing, and spiritual enlightenment and guidance. The flickering flame of a candle holds the key to unlocking your true potential in the realm of career and success. By harnessing the energy of candle magik, you can attract job opportunities and propel your career to new heights.

Candle magik rituals and spells have long been used to influence the course of one's professional life. The process begins by selecting a candle that resonates with your career goals. For those seeking success and recognition, a gold or yellow candle can be chosen, while a green candle can be used to attract abundance and financial prosperity. Once you have your candle, it's time to infuse it with your intentions.

Before lighting the candle, take a moment to visualize your desired outcome. Envision yourself excelling in your chosen field, receiving promotions, and attracting lucrative job offers. With each inhale, draw in the energy of success and ambition, and with each exhale, release any doubts or fears that may hinder your progress. As you light the candle, imagine the flame igniting the spark of opportunity within you.

To amplify the effects of your candle magik, consider incorporating other elements such as crystals, herbs, or sigils that align with your career goals. Citrine, known as the stone of abundance, can be placed near the candle to enhance financial success. Alternatively, anointing the candle with essential oils like bergamot or lavender can attract opportunities and promote confidence.

As the candle burns, allow the energy of your intentions to fill the space around you. Visualize the flame as a beacon, attracting job opportunities and career advancement towards you. Trust in the power of candle magik to align your path with success and take inspired action towards your goals.

Remember, candle magik is a tool that works in harmony with your own efforts. While the rituals and spells can open doors and create opportunities, it is crucial to actively seek out new avenues for career growth. Network, update your resume, and seize any chance to showcase your skills and talents.

By combining the power of candle magik with your own determination and effort, you can attract job opportunities and propel your career forward. Embrace the energy of success and watch as the universe conspires to bring you the professional fulfillment you deserve.

Enhancing Creativity and Productivity

In the realm of candle magic, the potential for enhancing creativity and productivity is not only possible but also highly accessible. By tapping into the power of candle rituals and spells, individuals interested in witchcraft, the occult, and magic can unlock their inner potential and manifest their creative energy in the most productive ways.

Candle magic rituals and spells provide a unique and powerful platform for igniting the creative spark within. Whether you are an artist seeking inspiration, a writer in need of fresh ideas, or simply looking to enhance your problem-solving abilities, candle magic can help you channel your creative energy and unleash your full potential.

For those seeking to enhance their love and relationships, candle magic rituals and spells can infuse romance, passion, and harmony into their lives. By selecting the right candles, utilizing specific colors, and performing rituals with intention, individuals can attract love, heal broken relationships, and deepen the connection with their partners.

In the realm of healing and wellness, candle magic rituals and spells can be a potent tool. By harnessing the energy of candles and combining them with healing intentions, individuals can promote physical, emotional, and spiritual well-being. Whether you are seeking relief from a specific ailment or looking to enhance your overall wellness, candle magic can serve as a powerful aid on your journey.

Prosperity and abundance are desires shared by many, and candle magic rituals and spells can assist in manifesting these desires. By selecting candles that symbolize wealth and abundance, and performing rituals with focus and intention, individuals can attract financial prosperity and opportunities for success.

Protection and cleansing are essential aspects of any spiritual practice, and candle magic rituals and spells can provide the necessary tools. By using specific candles and performing rituals with the intention of warding off negative energy and cleansing the aura, individuals can create a protective shield around themselves and their living spaces.

Manifestation and the law of attraction go hand in hand, and candle magic rituals and spells can be a powerful tool for bringing desires into reality. By selecting candles that align with specific intentions and performing rituals with unwavering belief, individuals can amplify their manifestation abilities and attract the life they desire.

For those seeking spiritual enlightenment and guidance, candle magic rituals and spells can serve as a pathway to higher realms. By utilizing candles and performing rituals with the intention of connecting with the divine, individuals can receive spiritual guidance, clarity, and a deeper understanding of their purpose.

Career and success are important aspects of our lives, and candle magic rituals and spells can be a valuable aid in achieving professional goals. By selecting candles that symbolize success, performing rituals with focus and intention, individuals can attract career opportunities, promotions, and the recognition they deserve.

Psychic development and intuition are skills that can be honed through candle magic rituals and spells. By utilizing candles and performing rituals with the intention of connecting with one's intuition and psychic abilities, individuals can enhance their spiritual gifts and gain deeper insights into themselves and the world around them.

Self-love and confidence are essential for personal growth and well-being, and candle magic rituals and spells can assist in cultivating these qualities. By selecting candles that symbolize self-love and performing rituals with the intention of boosting confidence and self-worth, individuals can enhance their sense of self and embrace their true potential.

Lastly, lunar and celestial energy play a significant role in candle magic rituals and spells. By aligning rituals with the phases of the moon and utilizing specific candles, individuals can harness the power of lunar and celestial energy to amplify their intentions and manifest their desires.

In conclusion, the realm of candle magic offers a wide range of rituals and spells that can enhance creativity and productivity. Whether you are seeking love, healing, prosperity, protection, manifestation, spiritual guidance, career success, psychic development, self-love, or lunar energy, candle magic rituals and spells can be a powerful tool in unlocking your inner potential and manifesting your desires. Embrace the art of candle magic and unlock the power within.

Overcoming Obstacles and Challenges in the Workplace

In the realm of candle magik, we often focus on harnessing the power of intention and manifestation to bring about positive changes in various aspects of our lives. However, it is important to acknowledge that obstacles and challenges are an inevitable part of our journey, including our professional endeavors. In this section, we will explore the ways in which candle magik can help us overcome these obstacles and thrive in the workplace.

One of the key principles of candle magik is the belief that our thoughts and intentions have the power to shape our reality. By utilizing this belief, we can create rituals and spells specifically designed to address the challenges we face in our careers. Whether it is dealing with difficult colleagues, a lack of motivation, or a stagnant career path, candle magik rituals and spells can serve as powerful tools for transformation.

In the workplace, relationships with colleagues and superiors play a significant role in our overall success and satisfaction. Candle magik rituals and spells focused on love and relationships can help us foster harmonious connections, resolve conflicts, and attract positive energy into our professional interactions.

Maintaining a healthy work-life balance is crucial for our overall well-being. By incorporating healing and wellness candle magik rituals and spells into our workplace routine, we can combat stress, promote self-care, and cultivate a positive work environment.

Financial stability and career growth are important aspects of our professional lives. By utilizing prosperity and abundance candle magik rituals and spells, we can align our energy with abundance, attract opportunities for financial prosperity, and manifest success in our chosen career paths.

In a competitive and sometimes toxic work environment, it is essential to protect ourselves from negative energies and entities. Protection and cleansing candle magik rituals and spells can create a shield of positive energy around us, warding off negativity and promoting a safe and nurturing workplace environment.

The law of attraction is a powerful force that can be harnessed to manifest our desires in the workplace. By employing manifestation and law of attraction candle magik rituals and spells, we can align our thoughts and intentions with our professional goals, attract success, and create opportunities for growth and advancement.

Connecting with our inner guidance and intuition is essential for making sound decisions in the workplace. Spiritual enlightenment and guidance candle magik rituals and spells can help us tap into our higher selves, gain clarity, and make choices that align with our true purpose and values.

Achieving career success requires dedication, focus, and

determination. Career and success candle magik rituals and spells can empower us to overcome obstacles, enhance our skills and talents, and attract opportunities that propel us towards our professional goals.

Developing our psychic abilities and intuition can provide valuable insights and guidance in the workplace. Psychic development and intuition candle magik rituals and spells can help us tap into our innate psychic abilities, enhance our intuitive skills, and make informed decisions in our professional lives.

Building self-love and confidence is crucial for navigating the challenges of the workplace. Self-love and confidence candle magik rituals and spells can help us release self-doubt, boost our self-esteem, and cultivate a positive mindset that empowers us to overcome any obstacles that come our way.

Harnessing the energy of the moon and celestial bodies can enhance the power of our candle magik rituals and spells in the workplace. Lunar and celestial energy candle magik rituals and spells can help us align with the cosmic energies, amplify our intentions, and bring about transformative changes in our professional lives.

By integrating these various aspects of candle magik into our approach to overcoming obstacles and challenges in the workplace, we can unlock our true potential and create a fulfilling and successful career. Remember, with the power of intention and the guidance of candle magik, no challenge is insurmountable. Embrace the magik within you and watch as your professional life transforms before your eyes.

Cultivating Leadership and Professional Skills

In the realm of witchcraft and the occult, it is essential to not only develop one's magical abilities but also to cultivate leadership and professional skills. The journey of becoming a powerful witch or practitioner of magik goes beyond spellcasting and rituals; it requires a well-rounded set of skills that can be applied to various aspects of life.

Leadership skills are crucial for those who wish to take charge of their own magical practice and guide others on their spiritual path. Effective communication, decision-making, and problem-solving are vital components of leadership. By honing these skills, witches and occult enthusiasts can confidently lead rituals, teach others, and provide guidance to those seeking their assistance.

Furthermore, professional skills are vital for those who wish to incorporate magik into their careers or offer their services to others. Whether it is creating and selling magikal products, providing tarot readings, or offering spiritual counseling, professionalism is key. This includes skills such as organization, time management, customer service, and marketing. Developing these skills ensures that one's magikal practice can be shared with others in a respectful and efficient manner.

To cultivate leadership and professional skills, it is essential to seek out opportunities for growth and development. Taking courses or workshops in leadership, communication, or business management can provide valuable knowledge and tools. Engaging in networking events within the witchcraft and occult communities can also offer opportunities to learn from experienced practitioners and exchange ideas with like-minded individuals.

Incorporating leadership and professional skills into specific niches of candle magik can open up new possibilities for practitioners. For example, those interested in love and relationships candle magik can utilize their leadership skills to guide others in creating rituals to attract or enhance romantic partnerships. Similarly, practitioners focusing on prosperity and abundance can use their professional skills to develop successful candle magik businesses or assist others in manifesting financial prosperity.

By cultivating leadership and professional skills, witches and practitioners of magik can elevate their practice to new heights. Not only will they have a deeper understanding of their craft, but they will also have the ability to inspire and guide others on their own magikal journeys. With a combination of magical prowess and strong leadership, the possibilities for personal and professional growth are endless in the world of witchcraft and the occult.

Creating a Successful and Fulfilling Career Path

In the realm of witchcraft and the occult, the pursuit of a successful and fulfilling career path is just as important as any other aspect of our lives. Our careers not only provide us with financial stability but also contribute to our personal growth and overall well-being. In this section, we will explore how candle magic can be used to enhance and manifest a career that aligns with our passions, values, and desires.

When it comes to candle magic rituals and spells for career and success, intention is paramount. Before embarking on any magical work, take the time to reflect on your career goals and aspirations. What kind of work ignites your passion? What skills and talents do you possess that can be utilized in your dream career? By gaining clarity on these aspects, you can direct your energy and focus towards manifesting the perfect career path.

One powerful ritual for career manifestation involves creating a sacred space where you can connect with your inner self and the divine energies. Start by selecting a candle that symbolizes success and abundance, such as a gold or green candle. Set up your ritual space with objects that inspire you and represent your desired career, such as a vision board or a symbol of the industry you wish to work in.

Light the chosen candle, allowing its flame to represent the spark of inspiration and the manifestation of your career goals. Visualize yourself excelling in your chosen field, feeling fulfilled and abundant. As the candle burns, repeat affirmations that resonate with your career intentions, such as "I am a successful and confident [career title]. Opportunities flow to me effortlessly, and I embrace them with gratitude."

While candle magic rituals can be potent tools for career manifestation, it is essential to remember that action is also necessary. Take practical steps towards your career goals, such as acquiring new skills, networking, and seeking mentorship. The combination of magical work and personal effort will create a powerful synergy that propels you towards your dream career.

In conclusion, candle magic rituals and spells can be powerful tools for creating a successful and fulfilling career path. By setting clear intentions, creating sacred space, and taking inspired action, you can align your energy with the career of your dreams. Remember, the key to a satisfying career lies within you, and with the guidance of candle magic, you can unlock the power to manifest your true potential.

CHAPTER ELEVEN

Unlocking and Developing Psychic Abilities

In the realm of candle magik, there lies a vast potential for unlocking and developing your psychic abilities. By harnessing the power of the flame, you can tap into your intuition, expand your psychic senses, and embark on a journey of self-discovery and spiritual growth.

Psychic abilities are not limited to a select few; they are innate within all of us. However, they often lay dormant, waiting to be awakened. Candle magik provides a powerful tool for awakening and strengthening these abilities, allowing you to connect with the unseen energies and realms that exist beyond our physical senses.

To begin unlocking your psychic potential, it is essential to cultivate a deep sense of inner stillness and focus. Through meditation and regular candle rituals, you can quiet the mind, open your heart, and create a sacred space for psychic development to flourish.

One effective method is to utilize specific candle colors and scents that correspond to psychic abilities. Purple candles, for example, are associated with intuition and spiritual insight, while white candles symbolize purity and clarity of thought. By incorporating these candles into your rituals, you can enhance your psychic receptivity and open yourself up to higher realms of consciousness.

In addition to candle selection, the practice of divination can also play a significant role in unlocking psychic abilities. Tarot cards, pendulums, and scrying mirrors can be used in conjunction with candle magik to strengthen your intuitive senses and receive messages from the spiritual realm.

Furthermore, it is crucial to trust your instincts and follow your intuition. As you engage in candle rituals, pay attention to any intuitive nudges or gut feelings that arise. These subtle whispers from your higher self and spirit guides can guide you towards unlocking your psychic potential.

Remember, psychic development is a gradual process. Be patient with yourself and allow your abilities to unfold naturally. As you continue to practice candle magik and explore the various realms of energy and spirituality, you will find that your psychic senses become sharper, your intuition becomes clearer, and your connection to the unseen becomes stronger.

Unlocking and developing your psychic abilities through candle magik is a transformative journey. As you delve deeper into the mysteries of the occult, you will discover a world of limitless possibilities and a heightened sense of self-awareness. Embrace the power within and let the flame guide you towards unlocking your full psychic potential.

Enhancing Intuition and Psychic Awareness

In the realm of magik and witchcraft, the power of intuition and psychic awareness is highly regarded and sought after. These abilities allow us to tap into the unseen energies and dimensions, providing us with valuable insights, guidance, and connection to the spiritual realm. In this section, we will explore various techniques and rituals within the realm of candle magik that can enhance your intuition and psychic abilities.

One of the most effective ways to enhance intuition is through meditation and mindfulness practices. By quieting the mind and turning inward, we can tune into our intuitive guidance and receive messages from the spiritual realm. Lighting a candle during meditation can help create a focused and sacred space, allowing you to connect with your higher self and the universal energies.

Another powerful tool for enhancing intuition is the use of specific herbs and essential oils. Incorporating these into your candle magik rituals can amplify your psychic awareness. Herbs such as lavender, mugwort, and rosemary have long been used for their psychic-enhancing properties. By infusing their essence into your candles or using them in combination with candle magik, you can strengthen your intuitive abilities.

Furthermore, working with crystals can also enhance psychic

118

awareness. Crystals such as amethyst, labradorite, and clear quartz are known for their ability to open and activate the third eye chakra, which is closely associated with intuition and psychic abilities. Placing these crystals near your candle or using them during meditation can help align and activate your intuitive powers.

In addition to these practices, it is crucial to cultivate a deep sense of trust and belief in your own intuition. Doubt and skepticism can hinder the development of psychic abilities. By acknowledging and embracing your inner knowing, you can strengthen your psychic connection and enhance your ability to receive messages and guidance.

Throughout this section, you will find specific candle magik rituals and spells that are designed to enhance your intuition and psychic awareness. Whether you are seeking to develop your clairvoyance, clairaudience, or clairsentience, these rituals will provide you with the tools and techniques to unlock your psychic potential.

Remember, the journey of enhancing intuition and psychic awareness is a personal one. Each individual has their unique strengths and abilities. Through dedication, practice, and an open heart, you can tap into the vast reservoir of wisdom and guidance that lies within.

Strengthening Divination Skills with Candle magik

In the mystical world of witchcraft and the occult, divination is an essential skill for those seeking guidance, insight, and connection with the spiritual realm. One powerful tool for enhancing your divination abilities is the practice of candle magik. By incorporating candles into your divination rituals and spells, you can unlock a deeper level of intuition and tap into the universal energies that surround you.

Candle magik rituals and spells have been used for centuries to manifest desires, heal emotional wounds, and attract positive energy into one's life. But did you know that candles can also be a potent tool for divination? By harnessing the energy and symbolism of candles, you can sharpen your psychic abilities and gain clarity in your spiritual journey.

Love and Relationships Candle Magic Rituals and Spells: Light a pink or red candle to attract love and enhance your romantic relationships. Use divination tools like tarot cards or scrying mirrors while focusing on the candle flame to gain insights into your love life.

Healing and Wellness Candle Magic Rituals and Spells: Utilize the soothing energy of candles to aid in physical and emotional healing. Light a blue or green candle and use divination techniques to uncover the root causes of any ailments or imbalances within your body and mind.

Prosperity and Abundance Candle Magic Rituals and Spells: Ignite a gold or green candle to attract wealth and abundance into your life. Enhance your divination skills by meditating on the candle's flame and visualize the financial opportunities that lie ahead.

Protection and Cleansing Candle Magic Rituals and Spells:

Shield yourself from negative energies and cleanse your aura by lighting a black or white candle. Engage in divination practices to identify any sources of negativity and seek guidance on how to protect yourself and your space.

Manifestation and Law of Attraction Candle Magic Rituals and Spells: Manifest your desires by lighting a yellow or orange candle. Combine divination techniques with candle magik to gain clarity on your goals and receive guidance on the necessary steps to manifest them.

Spiritual Enlightenment and Guidance Candle Magic Rituals and Spells: Connect with your higher self and seek spiritual guidance by lighting a purple or white candle. Engage in divination rituals to receive messages from the divine and gain insights into your spiritual path.

Career and Success Candle Magic Rituals and Spells: Light a green or gold candle to attract success and abundance in your career. Utilize divination tools to uncover any hidden opportunities or obstacles that may be affecting your professional growth.

Psychic Development and Intuition Candle Magic Rituals and Spells: Deepen your psychic abilities by incorporating purple or blue candles into your divination rituals. Meditate on the candle flame to enhance your intuition and receive clearer messages from the spiritual realm.

Self-Love and Confidence Candle Magic Rituals and Spells: Ignite a pink or yellow candle to cultivate self-love and boost your confidence. Combine divination practices with candle magik to gain insights into any self-limiting beliefs or patterns that may be holding you back.

Lunar and Celestial Energy Candle Magic Rituals and Spells: Harness the energy of the moon and stars by lighting a white or silver candle. Engage in divination rituals under the moonlight to receive celestial guidance and connect with the cosmic energies that surround you.

Incorporating candle magik into your divination practices can be a transformative experience, allowing you to tap into your innate psychic abilities and receive guidance from the spiritual realm. Experiment with different candle colors and divination tools to discover what resonates with you and deepens your connection to the mystical energies that surround us. Remember, the power lies within you, and candle magik is simply a tool to help unlock that power and strengthen your divination skills.

Connecting with the Spirit Realm and Higher Dimensions

In the world of candle magic, practitioners are often drawn to the idea of connecting with the spirit realm and higher dimensions. This section will explore the various techniques and rituals that can be used to establish a profound connection with these ethereal realms.

One of the fundamental principles of connecting with the spirit realm is the belief that we are not alone in this universe. There are beings and energies beyond our physical realm that can offer guidance, wisdom, and assistance. By developing a connection with these entities, practitioners can tap into a wellspring of knowledge and spiritual growth.

To initiate a connection with the spirit realm, it is important to create a sacred space. This can be achieved by setting up an altar or a designated area where you can focus your energy and intention. Surround yourself with items that resonate with the spiritual realm, such as crystals, feathers, or symbols that hold personal significance.

Candle magic can serve as a powerful tool to enhance your connection with the spirit realm. Begin by choosing a candle that symbolizes your intention, such as a white candle for purity and enlightenment or a purple candle for psychic development. As you light the candle, visualize a bridge forming between your physical world and the realms beyond. Feel the energy flowing through you, connecting you to the higher dimensions.

Meditation is another technique that can aid in connecting with the spirit realm. Find a quiet and comfortable space, and focus your attention on your breath. Allow your mind to enter a state of relaxation and receptivity. As you meditate, invite the spirits and beings from the higher dimensions to join you. Listen to any messages or guidance that may come through, and trust in the wisdom of these unseen forces.

It is important to approach the spirit realm with respect and reverence. Always remember to set clear intentions, establish boundaries, and protect yourself energetically. Use techniques such as grounding, shielding, and invoking protective energies to ensure a safe and positive connection.

By connecting with the spirit realm and higher dimensions, practitioners of candle magic can expand their consciousness, deepen their spiritual practice, and access profound insights and guidance. Embrace the mystery and wonder of these ethereal realms, and let the candle's flame illuminate your path to spiritual enlightenment.

Trusting Your Inner Guidance and Intuitive Insights

The practice of candle magic requires one to tap into their inner guidance and intuitive insights if they wish to harness its full power and potential. By learning to trust and embrace your inner knowing and intuition, you can greatly enhance the effectiveness of your rituals and spells, resulting in profound transformations in many different aspects of your life.

For those interested in witchcraft, the occult, and magik, understanding the importance of intuitive guidance is paramount. Your intuition is like a compass that guides you through the intricate web of energies that surround us. It is a deep knowing that goes beyond logic and rationality, allowing you to connect with the unseen forces that shape our reality.

When it comes to candle magik rituals and spells, trusting your inner guidance is particularly valuable. As you light your candles and set your intentions, pay attention to the subtle whispers within. Trust the sensations, hunches, and gut feelings that arise. These are your intuitive insights, guiding you towards the most effective ways to manifest your desires.

In the realm of love and relationships candle magik rituals and spells, your intuition can be a powerful tool. It can help you discern the right time to perform rituals, choose the appropriate colors and scents for your candles, and even guide you in attracting the right partner or nurturing an existing relationship.

Similarly, your intuition plays a vital role in healing and wellness candle magik rituals and spells. It can lead you to the specific herbs, oils, and crystals that resonate with your needs, allowing you to create a holistic and personalized healing experience.

In the realm of prosperity and abundance, your intuition can guide you to manifest financial stability and material success. By trusting your inner guidance, you can identify the blockages that hinder your prosperity and find the most effective candle magik rituals and spells to remove them.

Protection and cleansing candle magik rituals and spells are also enhanced by intuitive insights. Through your inner guidance, you can discover the most potent methods of shielding yourself from negative energies and purifying your space.

When it comes to manifestation and the law of attraction, your intuition can help you align your thoughts, emotions, and actions with your desires. By trusting your inner knowing, you can create powerful intentions and choose the appropriate candles and rituals to manifest your dreams.

In the pursuit of spiritual enlightenment and guidance, your intuition acts as a bridge between the physical and spiritual realms. It can guide you towards the practices, rituals, and candles that resonate with your spiritual journey, facilitating deep connections and profound transformations.

Career and success candle magik rituals and spells can benefit greatly from your intuitive insights. By trusting your inner guidance, you can identify the steps needed to advance in your career, attract opportunities, and manifest success.

Developing your psychic abilities and intuition is a fundamental aspect of candle magik. Through specific rituals and spells, you can enhance your intuitive powers, strengthen your connection to the spiritual realm, and unlock new levels of insight and wisdom.

Finally, self-love and confidence candle magik rituals and spells can be empowered by your intuition. By listening to your inner guidance, you can discover the self-care practices, affirmations, and rituals that cultivate self-love and boost your confidence.

Incorporating lunar and celestial energy into your candle magik rituals and spells is another way to enhance your intuitive abilities. By aligning your practice with the cycles of the moon and harnessing the energies of the celestial bodies, you can deepen your connection to the cosmos and tap into profound insights and guidance.

Trusting your inner guidance and intuitive insights in the realm of candle magik is a transformative journey. As you embrace your intuition, you unlock the full potential of your rituals and spells, inviting powerful and positive changes into your life.

CHAPTER TWELVE

Cultivating Self-Love and Acceptance

In the realm of candle magik, the practice of cultivating self-love and acceptance is of utmost importance. As individuals who are interested in witchcraft, the occult, and magik, we understand that true power lies within ourselves. By harnessing the energy of candle magik, we can unlock the power within and learn to love and accept ourselves fully.

Self-love is a journey that requires patience, compassion, and dedication. It is about honoring and embracing all aspects of ourselves, including our flaws and imperfections. Through the use of candle magik rituals and spells, we can create a sacred space that allows us to connect with our inner selves.

One powerful ritual to cultivate self-love and acceptance is the mirror meditation. Begin by lighting a candle that resonates with self-love and placing it in front of a mirror. Sit comfortably in front of the mirror and gaze into your own eyes, allowing yourself to truly see and acknowledge the person staring back at you.

As you connect with your reflection, affirmations can be a powerful tool. Repeat positive affirmations such as "I am worthy of love and acceptance," "I embrace my true self," and "I am enough" while maintaining eye contact with your reflection. Visualize these affirmations sinking deep into your subconscious, replacing any self-doubt or negativity.

Incorporating essential oils or herbs that promote self-love and acceptance can enhance the power of your candle magik rituals. Rose, lavender, and jasmine are all excellent choices. You can anoint your candle with the oil or sprinkle dried herbs around the candle as you perform your ritual.

Remember, self-love is not selfish; it is a necessary act of self-care. By embracing and accepting ourselves, we create a solid foundation for personal growth and fulfillment. Through the practice of candle magik, we can cultivate a deep sense of self-love and confidence that will radiate outwards, positively impacting all areas of our lives.

In the pages that follow, you will find a variety of candle magik rituals and spells specifically designed to enhance self-love and confidence. Whether you are seeking to heal past wounds, boost your self-esteem, or simply embrace your authentic self, these rituals will guide you on your journey of self-discovery and empowerment.

By incorporating these rituals into your practice, you will not only unlock the power within but also unlock the power of self-love and acceptance. Embrace the magik that lies within you and watch as your life transforms in beautiful and unexpected ways.

Healing and Releasing Self-Doubt and Insecurities

In our journey towards self-discovery and empowerment, we often encounter self-doubt and insecurities that hold us back from reaching our fullest potential. These negative emotions can be debilitating, hindering our progress and preventing us from embracing the magic within us. However, the power of candle magik can help us heal and release these limiting beliefs, allowing us to embrace our true essence and step into our power.

Candle magik rituals and spells have been used for centuries to harness the energy of fire and transform it into a powerful tool for manifestation. By incorporating specific herbs, colors, and intentions, we can create a sacred space that supports our journey towards self-healing and self-acceptance.

To begin the process of healing and releasing self-doubt and insecurities, start by selecting a candle that resonates with your intention. For this particular ritual, a white or light blue candle would be ideal, symbolizing purity and clarity. As you light the candle, visualize the flame as a beacon of light that illuminates your path towards self-love and confidence.

Next, create a safe and serene environment by cleansing your space with sage or palo santo. As the smoke purifies the room, visualize it clearing away any negative energy or self-doubt that surrounds you.

Now, take a moment to connect with your inner self. Close your eyes and take deep breaths, allowing yourself to release any tension or anxiety that may be weighing you down. As you exhale, visualize the doubts and insecurities leaving your body, evaporating into the ether.

Once you feel centered and grounded, write down the affirmations that resonate with your journey towards self-acceptance. For example, "I am worthy of love and success," or "I release all self-doubt and embrace my true potential." Infuse these affirmations with your intention and belief, knowing that by repeating them, you are shifting your mindset and embracing a new reality.

Place the written affirmations beneath the candle, allowing the flame to infuse them with its transformative energy. As the candle burns, visualize the doubts and insecurities dissolving, being replaced by a sense of self-assurance and confidence.

Finally, express gratitude for the healing and transformation that is taking place within you. Thank the universe, your guides, and yourself for the courage to confront and release these limiting beliefs.

Repeat this ritual as often as needed, allowing the candle magik to guide you on your journey towards self-love and confidence. Remember, you have the power to heal and release self-doubt and insecurities. Embrace the magic within you and watch as your true essence shines brighter than ever before.

Boosting Self-Confidence and Empowerment

If you are interested in the world of witchcraft and the occult, you should know that self-confidence and empowerment play a crucial role in personal growth and success. When we believe in ourselves and harness our inner power, we can achieve great things and manifest our desires through the practice of candle magic. This section will explore various candle magic rituals and spells specifically designed to boost self-confidence and empower individuals on their spiritual journey.

Candle magic is a powerful tool for self-transformation and can significantly impact our mindset and belief system. By incorporating candle rituals into our daily routine, we can cultivate a strong sense of self-love and confidence. The flickering flame represents the spark within us, illuminating our path towards empowerment.

One powerful ritual to boost self-confidence involves selecting a candle in a color that resonates with your intention. Light the candle and visualize yourself radiating with confidence and empowerment. As the flame burns, imagine any self-doubt or insecurities being transformed into unwavering self-assurance. Repeat positive affirmations, such as "I am confident and capable" to reinforce your belief in yourself. (Check the other lists of affirmations I have given you).

Another technique is to create a self-empowerment sigil, a unique symbol representing your personal power and strength. Carve the sigil onto a candle and anoint it with an empowering oil, such as rosemary or patchouli. As the candle burns, focus on the sigil and visualize it infusing you with confidence and empowerment. This ritual can be performed during moments of self-doubt or before important events, providing a boost of inner strength.

Additionally, incorporating lunar and celestial energy into candle magic rituals can further enhance self-confidence and empowerment. During the waxing moon phase, when the moon is growing in illumination, perform a ritual to harness the energy of expansion and growth. Light a candle and visualize your confidence blossoming alongside the moon's increasing brightness. Meditate on the moon's radiant energy infusing you with self-assurance and empowerment.

By regularly practicing these candle magic rituals and spells, individuals interested in witchcraft, the occult, and magik can unlock their inner power, boost self-confidence, and empower themselves on their spiritual journey. Remember, you possess the ability to manifest your desires and create a life filled with confidence, abundance, and success. Embrace the power of candle magic and watch as your self-confidence soars to new heights.

Embracing Your Authentic Self

In the mystical realm of candle magic, there is a powerful tool that can help you unlock your true potential. By embracing your authentic self, you can tap into the limitless power within you and manifest your desires with intention and clarity. This section delves into the profound practice of embracing your authentic self through candle magic rituals and spells.

For those interested in witchcraft, the occult, and magic, understanding and accepting your authentic self is a crucial step in harnessing the full potential of your magical abilities. By recognizing and embracing your unique gifts, talents, and desires, you can align your intentions with the universe and manifest your dreams in a more authentic and powerful way.

Whether you seek love and relationships, healing and wellness, prosperity and abundance, protection and cleansing, manifestation and the law of attraction, spiritual enlightenment and guidance, career and success, psychic development and intuition, self-love and confidence, or lunar and celestial energy, candle magic rituals and spells can assist you on your journey.

Through the art of candle magic, you can create sacred spaces and rituals that allow you to connect with your true self on a deeper level. By incorporating specific colors, scents, symbols, and intentions into your candle magic practice, you can amplify your manifestation abilities and bring your desires into reality.

This section explores various candle magic rituals and spells tailored to each niche, providing step-by-step instructions and insights to help you embrace your authentic self in different areas of your life. Whether you're seeking guidance in your career, healing for your body and mind, or love and abundance in your relationships, these rituals will empower you to tap into your true potential and create the life you desire.

Remember, embracing your authentic self is a lifelong journey. As you explore the realms of candle magic and unlock the power within, you will discover new facets of your true self and continue to strengthen and grow. Embrace the magic within you and let your authentic self shine brightly in all aspects of your life.

Nurturing Self-Care and Inner Beauty

When it comes to the art of candle magic, it is imperative that we not only concentrate on achieving external goals and fulfilling our desires, but also on taking care of our inner selves, cultivating a sense of inner peace and harmony. Self-care and inner beauty are crucial aspects that contribute to our overall well-being and success in any area of life. By dedicating time and energy to our own self-love and confidence, we cultivate a strong foundation from which to manifest our desires and connect with the surrounding energies.

One of the most powerful aspects of candle magic is its ability to serve as a tool for self-reflection and personal growth. Through the practice of candle magic rituals and spells, we can embark on a journey of self-discovery and self-care. By setting intentions and working with specific candle colors, herbs, and oils, we can create a sacred space to nurture ourselves and enhance our inner beauty.

Self-love and confidence are foundational elements that empower us to pursue our dreams and desires. In the realm of candle magic, we can harness the energy of self-love and confidence by incorporating specific rituals and spells into our practice. Lighting a red candle to ignite our passion and self-confidence or a pink candle to enhance self-love and compassion can help us connect with our inner power and radiate beauty from within.

Candle magic can be a powerful tool for healing and wellness. By incorporating specific rituals and spells into our self-care routines, we can support our physical, emotional, and spiritual well-being. Whether it is lighting a green candle to promote healing and abundance or a blue candle to facilitate emotional healing and inner peace, candle magic rituals can serve as a catalyst for positive transformation and holistic well-being.

When we prioritize self-care and inner beauty, we create a solid foundation for success in all areas of life. By dedicating time and energy to nurturing ourselves through candle magic rituals and spells, we can cultivate self-love, confidence, and a deep sense of inner beauty. As we align with our true selves and connect with the energies of the universe, we open ourselves up to endless possibilities for growth, happiness, and fulfillment.

CHAPTER THIRTEEN

Harnessing the Power of the Moon in Candle magik

When it comes to candle magik, the moon is considered as an incredibly powerful and energetic celestial entity within its realm. The moon's phases, from waxing to full to waning, can influence the outcomes of our rituals and spells. By understanding and using the lunar energy in our candle magik practices, we can enhance the effectiveness of our intentions and manifest our desires more easily. This is why I have the moon cycles in the back of this book. It's important to know when these events are happening when you are working magik. Any magik, not just candle magik.

During the waxing moon, when the moon is growing in size, it is a perfect time for initiating new projects and setting intentions for growth and abundance. This phase is ideal for rituals and spells related to prosperity, career success, and manifestation. By lighting a candle that corresponds to our intention, we can create a focused energy and direct it towards our goals.

As the moon reaches its fullness, its energy is at its peak, making it a powerful time for love and relationships. The full moon radiates a strong energy of attraction and passion, making it an opportune time for love spells and rituals to strengthen existing relationships. By incorporating candles that symbolize love and romance, we can amplify the energy and draw love into our lives.

The waning moon, when the moon is decreasing in size, is associated with release and cleansing. This phase is perfect for protection and cleansing rituals, removing negative energy, and banishing unwanted influences from our lives. By using candles that represent purification and protection, we can harness the moon's energy to create a shield of spiritual light around us.

In addition to the moon's phases, specific lunar events such as eclipses and full moon rituals can further amplify our candle magik practices. Eclipses are known for their intense energy, allowing us to tap into the hidden depths of our subconscious mind and manifest profound transformations. Full moon rituals, on the other hand, provide an opportunity for spiritual enlightenment and guidance. By incorporating candles that correspond to lunar events, we can align ourselves with their unique energies and achieve remarkable results.

Remember, as practitioners of candle magik, it is essential to respect the natural cycles of the moon and work in harmony with its energy. By understanding and harnessing the power of the moon, we can enhance our candle magik rituals and spells in various aspects of life, including love and relationships, healing and wellness, prosperity and abundance, protection and cleansing, manifestation and law of attraction, spiritual enlightenment and guidance, career and success, psychic development and intuition, self-love and confidence, and lunar and celestial energy. The moon is a magnificent ally on our magikal journey, supporting us as we unlock the power within ourselves.

Working with Planetary Energies for magikal Intentions

Utilizing the power of planetary energies is a key aspect of candle magik, as it can greatly increase the potency of your spells and rituals. Each planet in our solar system carries its own unique energy and symbolism, which can be utilized to manifest your intentions with greater precision and potency. Whether you are seeking love and relationships, healing and wellness, prosperity and abundance, protection and cleansing, manifestation and law of attraction, spiritual enlightenment and guidance, career and success, psychic development and intuition, self-love and confidence, or lunar and celestial energy, understanding how to work with planetary energies is a valuable tool in your magikal arsenal.

The planets and their corresponding energies can be aligned with specific candle colors, scents, and corresponding intentions. For example, Venus, the planet of love and relationships, can be invoked through the use of pink or red candles, adorned with rose or jasmine scents. This combination can amplify your intentions to attract a soulmate or enhance the love and passion in an existing relationship.

Similarly, the healing and wellness properties of the Moon can be harnessed through white or silver candles, accompanied by lavender or eucalyptus scents. This combination can aid in physical, emotional, and spiritual healing, promoting overall well-being.

To manifest abundance and prosperity, align your intentions with the energy of Jupiter. Utilize green or gold candles, and infuse them with the fragrances of cinnamon or clove. This combination can attract financial success, opportunities, and material abundance.

When it comes to protection and cleansing, the energy of Saturn can be invoked. Black or dark blue candles, combined with myrrh or frankincense scents, can create a powerful shield against negative energies, hexes, and psychic attacks.

To work with the energy of the Sun, which governs manifestation and the law of attraction, opt for yellow or orange candles. Enhance their power with the scents of citrus or sandalwood. This combination can amplify your ability to manifest your desires and attract positive outcomes.

By understanding the unique energies associated with each planet, you can tailor your candle magik rituals and spells to align with your specific intentions. Whether you seek spiritual enlightenment, career success, psychic development, self-love, or the energy of the moon and celestial bodies, working with planetary energies can unlock the full potential of your magikal practice. Embrace the power of the planets and watch as your intentions manifest with ease and grace.

Lunar Rituals for Emotional Healing and Transformation

The moon's power is an essential element in the realm of candle magik and should not be overlooked. The moon's energy, being intertwined with our emotions and subconscious mind, is a force of great potency that can bring about healing and transformation. The purpose of this section is to examine different lunar rituals that can be utilized to help you take advantage of the moon's energy for the purpose of experiencing emotional healing, personal growth, and spiritual transformation.

1. *The New Moon Ritual for Emotional Release*: The new moon symbolizes new beginnings and fresh starts. This ritual

focuses on releasing emotional baggage and setting intentions for emotional healing. Light a white candle during the new moon, and as it burns, visualize releasing any negative emotions or past traumas. Write down these emotions on a piece of paper and burn it in the candle flame, affirming your intention for emotional healing and transformation.

2. *Full Moon Ritual for Self-Love and Empowerment*: The full moon represents abundance and illumination. This ritual focuses on cultivating self-love and empowerment. Begin by lighting a pink candle, symbolizing love and compassion. As you gaze at the candle flame, affirm positive affirmations about yourself and your worthiness. Write down any self-limiting beliefs on a piece of paper and burn it in the candle flame, releasing them into the universe and welcoming self-love and empowerment.

3. *Waxing Moon Ritual for Emotional Growth:* The waxing moon is a time of growth and manifestation. This ritual is designed to support emotional growth and personal development. Light a green candle, representing growth and abundance. As the candle burns, meditate on areas of your life where emotional growth is needed. Visualize yourself overcoming emotional challenges and becoming stronger. Write down your intentions for emotional growth and place it under the candle. Allow the candle to burn out completely, symbolizing the manifestation of your emotional growth.

4. *Waning Moon Ritual for Letting Go:* The waning moon signifies release and letting go. This ritual focuses on releasing negative emotions and patterns that no longer serve you. Light a

black candle to symbolize the release of negativity. As it burns, visualize all negative emotions and patterns being dissolved and transmuted into positive energy. Write down what you wish to let go of and burn it in the candle flame. Affirm your intention to let go and invite emotional healing and transformation into your life.

Harnessing the lunar energy through candle magik can be a powerful tool for emotional healing and transformation. By aligning your intentions with the phases of the moon, you can unlock the moon's energy and bring profound changes into your life. Remember, consistency and genuine belief in the power of these rituals are key to manifesting emotional healing and transformation. Embrace the lunar energy and watch as it guides you on a journey of emotional growth and empowerment.

Celestial Alignments and their Influence in Candle magik

The impact of celestial alignments on the outcome of rituals and spells in the realm of candle magic is considered to be of great significance. By utilizing the unique energies present in the celestial bodies, such as the moon and planets, one can enhance the effectiveness and power of candle magik.

The moon, in particular, plays a vital role in candle magik rituals and spells. Its phases are connected to various aspects of our lives, and by aligning our intentions with the corresponding lunar energy, we can amplify the desired outcome. For instance, during the waxing moon phase, when the moon is growing fuller, it is a suitable time for manifestation and attracting abundance. Lighting a candle during this phase and focusing on your desires can help manifest your goals more effectively.

Similarly, the different zodiac signs and planetary movements also influence candle magik rituals and spells. Each zodiac sign and planet carries unique energies that can be utilized for specific purposes. For example, if you are seeking love and relationships, performing a candle magik ritual during Venus' alignment can enhance the potency of your intentions, as Venus is associated with love and romance.

Moreover, planetary retrogrades can also impact candle magik rituals. Retrogrades are periods when planets appear to move backward in their orbit, and they are believed to create a shift in energy. During retrogrades, it is advisable to focus on introspection, releasing negative patterns, and reassessing goals. By incorporating specific candles and intentions aligned with the retrograde energy, you can optimize your candle magik practice.

Understanding and working with celestial alignments in candle magik can open up a world of possibilities for practitioners. By attuning ourselves to the energies of the moon, planets, and other celestial bodies, we can enhance the power of our intentions and create positive changes in various aspects of our lives.

Whether you are seeking love and relationships, healing and wellness, prosperity and abundance, protection and cleansing, or any other area of focus, incorporating celestial energy into your candle magik rituals and spells can amplify your results. By aligning with the natural rhythms of the universe, you can tap into greater spiritual enlightenment, guidance, and success.

Amplifying Magikal Energy with Lunar and Celestial Practices

For many years, practitioners in the realm of witchcraft and the occult have acknowledged the potency of tapping into lunar and celestial energy to intensify their magikal workings. The moon, a celestial body that has been observed since ancient times, continues to hold a special significance in many traditions across the globe due to its ever-changing phases. This natural satellite's energy can be harnessed as a powerful tool by those seeking to enhance their candle magik rituals and spells, allowing them to tap into the moon's vast and mysterious power.

The moon's influence on our emotions and energy is undeniable. Just as the tides are affected by its gravitational pull, so too are our own energies influenced by the moon's phases. By aligning our candle magik rituals and spells with the moon's cycles, we can tap into this celestial energy and amplify our intentions.

The New Moon is a time of new beginnings and fresh starts, making it an ideal phase for setting intentions and manifesting desires. Light a candle representing your goal or desire, and as you focus on the flame, visualize your intention taking shape. The energy of the New Moon will support your manifestation efforts and help bring your desires into fruition.

As the moon waxes and grows in illumination, so does our ability to attract abundance and prosperity. During this phase, candle magik rituals and spells focused on financial growth and material success can be particularly potent. Choose a green or gold candle to represent wealth and abundance, and infuse it with your intentions. Burn the candle as you visualize yourself surrounded by prosperity, allowing the energy of the waxing moon to amplify your desires.

The Full Moon is a time of heightened energy and power, making it ideal for rituals and spells that require a strong burst of energy. Love and relationship spells, healing and wellness rituals, and spells for protection and cleansing are especially potent during this phase. Utilize the full moon's energy to amplify your intentions and bring about positive transformations in these areas of your life.

Additionally, celestial events such as meteor showers or planetary alignments can provide unique opportunities to tap into the magikal energy of the cosmos. By incorporating these events into your candle magik rituals and spells, you can infuse your intentions with the amplified energy of the celestial bodies.

Remember, while harnessing lunar and celestial energy can greatly enhance your candle magik practices, it is important to always approach these rituals with respect and mindfulness. Tune in to your intuition and work with the energy that resonates most strongly with you. Through the alignment of your intentions, candle magik, and the powerful energy of the moon and celestial bodies, you have the ability to unlock the hidden potential within and manifest your desires with greater ease and efficacy.

CHAPTER FOURTEEN

Making Candles

If you don't have access to a decently stocked store, you can make a candle for a particular purpose. The big advantage to this is that you can incorporate oils and finely ground herbs to super charge the candle for most any purpose.

I have used white wax with pumpkin spice mixed in to act as a money draw candle. It worked. Didn't smell like pumpkin spice, but it still did the job. Making a money drawing candle is a great way to bring abundance and prosperity into your life. You can use any scent that you associate with positive energy, such as citrus, cinnamon, or jasmine.

The most important thing is to mix the wax with a money drawing oil such as patchouli or cinnamon. It is also a good idea to write your intention on the candle before you light it. Visualize what you are asking for and focus on that while you light it.

Believe that your wish will come true and let the candle do its work.

You will encounter several choices for the base wax. My personal favorite was beeswax, which burned cleaner than paraffin wax. It gave a nice scent, and it was easier to work with than paraffin. It was more Eco-friendly than paraffin wax. However, if you are looking for a cheaper alternative, paraffin wax is still a great choice.

You will also need a double-boiler and one pot or pan to sacrifice for making the candles.

A trip to a hobby and craft store will give you the opportunity to explore the choices of molds and dyes.

Materials

-Wax: You can use either paraffin or soy wax.

-Wicks: These will come with the wax or can be purchased separately.

-Fragrance: Fragrance oils are used to scent the candles.

-Dye: This is needed to match the color to your desire. Refer to the candle color chart at the end of the book.

-Molds: Candle molds are used to shape the candles into whatever shape you'd like.

-Thermometer: This is used to track the temperature of the wax as it melts.

-Glue Dots: These are used to secure the wick to the bottom of the mold.

-Oils as needed

-Tools: You will need a spoon or a knife to stir the wax and a pair of scissors to cut the wick.

Making Candles for Magik

Choose the color and purpose for your candles. Such as green for wealth and abundance. Then to the wax, also add oils to enhance the magik, powered herbs, and lots of intent.

Be careful adding whole herbs, as the plant material can act as a second wick, causing the candle to burn much faster and possibly catch fire. When adding ground or powered herbs, be sure to only add a small amount and spread it out evenly. This will help keep the candle burning at a safe rate and help prevent any potential fire hazards. Always be sure to use a heat-safe container for burning candles and keep it away from any flammable materials. A list of oils and herbs is in the Appendix of this book.

A few combinations that have worked for me follows:

- Green with basil and cinnamon, for attracting money safely.
- Pink with rose oil to attract a lover or partner.
- Blue with frankincense oil for purifying a space.
- Yellow with bay leaves to open up paths of communication.

This list is just a start. I want you to begin to explore the combinations and see what works best for you!

It's easy to make candles, you can even begin by purchasing a kit. Make sure the kit contains the dyes in the colors you wish to use. I have found that even a couple of crayons added to the wax will produce rich colors.

I have made candles with the stiff wicks that have wire inside, and these work best for the larger pillar candles I needed.

As the candle cools in the mold, the wax will sink in, shrinking as it cools. At that point, reheat the wax and top off the mold. You'll need to repeat this as often as needed until the candle is filled in. After releasing the candle from the mold, you will need to level the base so that it stands straight. I would do this by heating a small, cheap pan and pressing the candle onto the hot surface. Then allow it to cool.

Use a release spray to make removing the finished candle easier. Get the spray at your local hobby shop. Some shops have a limited supply of candle making supplies, so you may need to shop online.

CHAPTER FIFTEEN

Reflecting on Your Candle Magik Journey

Candle magik is a powerful tool that allows you to harness the energy of fire and combine it with your intentions to manifest your desires. Throughout this book, you have explored various aspects of candle magik, from love and relationships to healing and wellness, prosperity and abundance to protection and cleansing, and many more.

During your journey, you have hopefully learned to set clear intentions, choose the right candles and colors, and create the perfect environment for your rituals. You have witnessed the power of visualization, meditation, and affirmation as you focused your energy and directed it towards your goals. Make sure to check the appendix and the references I have made available to you.

Now, as you reflect on your candle magik journey, consider the changes you have seen in your life. Have you experienced an improvement in your relationships? Has your health and well-being taken a positive turn? Have you noticed an increase in prosperity and abundance? Note these transformations and celebrate your achievements.

It is also important to acknowledge any challenges or obstacles you may have encountered along the way. Candle magik is not always a smooth path, and it requires dedication and perseverance. Reflect on the lessons you have learned and how they have shaped your journey. Embrace the growth and wisdom that have come from these experiences.

As you move forward, continue to incorporate candle magik into your daily life. Whether it is for spiritual enlightenment, guidance, career and success, or self-love and confidence, let candle magik be a constant companion on your path. Explore the mystical energies of the moon and celestial bodies, and tap into the power they offer to enhance your rituals.

Remember, your candle magik journey is not a destination but an ongoing process of self-discovery and transformation. Reflect regularly and reassess your goals and desires. Allow yourself to develop and adapt as you deepen your understanding of this ancient art.

May your candle magik journey continue to illuminate your path and bring forth the manifestations you seek. Embrace the power within you and let it guide you towards a life filled with love, abundance, and spiritual growth.

Appendix

Time conversion website: https://www.worldtimebuddy.com

Download a PDF of this chart here:

https://davepsychic.com/candle-magik-for-everyone-calendar/

Moon Cycles, 2023 - 2030

Lunar Phase	Date & Time — America/New York		UTC Date & Time	
Bring begins	Jan 6, Fri	06:09 PM	Jan 6, Fri	11:09 PM
Release begins	Jan 21, Sat	03:55 PM	Jan 21, Sat	08:55 PM
Bring begins	Feb 5, Sun	01:30 PM	Feb 5, Sun	06:30 PM
Release begins	Feb 20, Mon	02:09 AM	Feb 20, Mon	07:09 AM
Bring begins	Mar 7, Tue	07:42 AM	Mar 7, Tue	12:42 PM
Release begins	Mar 21, Tue	01:26 PM	Mar 21, Tue	05:26 PM
Bring begins	Apr 6, Thu	12:37 AM	Apr 6, Thu	04:37 AM
Release begins	Apr 20, Thu	12:15 AM	Apr 20, Thu	04:15 AM
Bring begins	May 5, Fri	01:36 PM	May 5, Fri	05:36 PM
Release begins	May 19, Fri	11:55 AM	May 19, Fri	03:55 PM

Bring begins	Jun 3, Sat	11:43 PM	Jun 4, Sun	03:43 AM
Release begins	Jun 18, Sun	12:39 AM	Jun 18, Sun	04:39 AM
Bring begins	Jul 3, Mon	07:40 AM	Jul 3, Mon	11:40 AM
Release begins	Jul 17, Mon	02:33 PM	Jul 17, Mon	06:33 PM
Bring begins	Aug 1, Tue	02:33 PM	Aug 1, Tue	06:33 PM
Release begins	Aug16, Wed	05:38 AM	Aug 16, Wed	09:38 AM
Bring begins	Aug 30, Wed	09:37 PM	Aug 31, Thu	01:37 AM
Release begins	Sep 14, Thu	09:40 PM	Sep 15, Fri	01:40 AM
Bring begins	Sep 29, Fri	05:58 AM	Sep 29, Fri	09:58 AM
Release begins	Oct 14, Sat	01:55 PM	Oct 14, Sat	05:55 PM
Bring begins	Oct 28, Sat	04:24 PM	Oct 28, Sat	08:24 PM
Release begins	Nov 13, Mon	04:27 AM	Nov 13, Mon	09:27 AM
Bring begins	Nov 27, Mon	04:16 AM	Nov 27, Mon	09:16 AM
Release begins	Dec 12, Tue	06:32 PM	Dec 12, Tue	11:32 PM
Bring begins	Dec 26, Tue	07:33 PM	Dec 27, Wed	12:33 AM

2024

Lunar Phase

	Date & Time America/New York		UTC Date & Time	
Release begins	Jan 11, Thu	06:58 AM	Jan 11, Thu	11:58 AM

152

Bring begins	Jan 25, Thu	12:54 PM	Jan 25, Thu	05:54 PM
Release begins	Feb 9, Fri	06:00 PM	Feb 9, Fri	11:00 PM
Bring begins	Feb 24, Sat	07:31 AM	Feb 24, Sat	12:31 PM
Release begins	Mar 10, Sun	05:02 AM	Mar 10, Sun	09:02 AM
Bring begins	Mar 25, Mon	03:01 AM	Mar 25, Mon	07:01 AM
Release begins	Apr 8, Mon	02:23 PM	Apr 8, Mon	06:23 PM
Bring begins	Apr 23, Tue	07:51 PM	Apr 23, Tue	11:51 PM
Release begins	May 7, Tue	11:24 PM	May 8, Wed	03:24 AM
Bring begins	May 23, Thu	09:55 AM	May 23, Thu	01:55 PM
Release begins	Jun 6, Thu	08:40 AM	Jun 6, Thu	12:40 PM
Bring begins	Jun 21, Fri	09:10 PM	Jun 22, Sat	01:10 AM
Release begins	Jul 5, Fri	06:59 PM	Jul 5, Fri	10:59 PM
Bring begins	Jul 21, Sun	06:19 AM	Jul 21, Sun	10:19 AM
Release begins	Aug 4, Sun	07:14 AM	Aug 4, Sun	11:14 AM
Bring begins	Aug 19, Mon	02:28 PM	Aug 19, Mon	06:28 PM
Release begins	Sep 2, Mon	09:56 PM	Sep 3, Tue	01:56 AM
Bring begins	Sep 17, Tue	10:36 PM	Sep 18, Wed	02:36 AM
Release begins	Oct 2, Wed	02:50 PM	Oct 2, Wed	06:50 PM
Bring begins	Oct 17, Thu	07:27 AM	Oct 17, Thu	11:27 AM
Release begins	Nov 1, Fri	08:48 AM	Nov 1, Fri	12:48 PM

Bring begins	Nov 15, Fri	04:29 PM	Nov 15, Fri	09:29 PM
Release begins	Dec 1, Sun	01:22 AM	Dec 1, Sun	06:22 AM
Bring begins	Dec 15, Sun	04:02 AM	Dec 15, Sun	09:02 AM
Release begins	Dec 30, Mon	05:27 PM	Dec 30, Mon	10:27 PM

2025

Lunar Phase UTC Date & Time			Local Date & Time America/New York	
Bring begins	Jan 13, Mon	05:27 PM	Jan 13, Mon	10:27 PM
Release begins	Jan 29, Wed	07:37 AM	Jan 29, Wed	12:37 PM
Bring begins	Feb 12, Wed	08:54 AM	Feb 12, Wed	01:54 PM
Release begins	Feb 27, Thu	07:46 PM	Feb 28, Fri	12:46 AM
Bring begins	Mar 14, Fri	02:55 AM	Mar 14, Fri	06:55 AM
Release begins	Mar 29, Sat	07:00 AM	Mar 29, Sat	11:00 AM
Bring begins	Apr 12, Sat	08:23 PM	Apr 13, Sun	12:23 AM
Release begins	Apr 27, Sun	03:33 PM	Apr 27, Sun	07:33 PM
Bring begins	May 12, Mon	12:58 PM	May 12, Mon	04:58 PM
Release begins	May 26, Mon	11:04 PM	May 27, Tue	03:04 AM
Bring begins	Jun 11, Wed	03:46 AM	Jun 11, Wed	07:46 AM
Release begins	Jun 25, Wed	06:33 AM	Jun 25, Wed	10:33 AM

Bring begins	Jul 10, Thu	04:38 PM	Jul 10, Thu	08:38 PM
Release begins	Jul 24, Thu	03:12 PM	Jul 24, Thu	07:12 PM
Bring begins	Aug 9, Sat	03:57 AM	Aug 9, Sat	07:57 AM
Release begins	Aug 23, Sat	02:07 AM	Aug 23, Sat	06:07 AM
Bring begins	Sep 7, Sun	02:10 PM	Sep 7, Sun	06:10 PM
Release begins	Sep 21, Sun	03:54 PM	Sep 21, Sun	07:54 PM
Bring begins	Oct 6, Mon	11:48 PM	Oct 7, Tue	03:48 AM
Release begins	Oct 21, Tue	08:25 AM	Oct 21, Tue	12:25 PM
Bring begins	Nov 5, Wed	08:20 AM	Nov 5, Wed	01:20 PM
Release begins	Nov 20, Thu	01:48 AM	Nov 20, Thu	06:48 AM
Bring begins	Dec 4, Thu	06:15 PM	Dec 4, Thu	11:15 PM
Release begins	Dec 19, Fri	08:44 PM	Dec 20, Sat	01:44 AM

2026

Lunar Phase	Date & Time America/New York		UTC Date & Time	
Bring begins	Jan 3, Sat	05:04 AM	Jan 3, Sat	10:04 AM
Release begins	Jan 18, Sun	02:53 PM	Jan 18, Sun	07:53 PM
Bring begins	Feb 1, Sun	05:10 PM	Feb 1, Sun	10:10 PM
Release begins	Feb 17, Tue	07:03 AM	Feb 17, Tue	12:03 PM
Bring begins	Mar 3, Tue	06:39 AM	Mar 3, Tue	11:39 AM
Release begins	Mar 18, Wed	09:26 PM	Mar 19, Thu	01:26 AM
Bring begins	Apr 1, Wed	10:13 PM	Apr 2, Thu	02:13 AM

Release begins	Apr 17, Fri	07:54 AM	Apr 17, Fri	11:54 AM
Bring begins	May 1, Fri	01:24 PM	May 1, Fri	05:24 PM
Release begins	May 16, Sat	04:03 PM	May 16, Sat	08:03 PM
Bring begins	May 31, Sun	04:46 AM	May 31, Sun	08:46 AM
Release begins	Jun 14, Sun	10:56 PM	Jun 15, Mon	02:56 AM
Bring begins	Jun 29, Mon	07:58 PM	Jun 29, Mon	11:58 PM
Release begins	Jul 14, Tue	05:45 AM	Jul 14, Tue	09:45 AM
Bring begins	Jul 29, Wed	10:37 AM	Jul 29, Wed	02:37 PM
Release begins	Aug 12, Wed	01:37 PM	Aug 12, Wed	05:37 PM
Bring begins	Aug 28, Fri	12:19 AM	Aug 28, Fri	04:19 AM
Release begins	Sep 10, Thu	11:27 PM	Sep 11, Fri	03:27 AM
Bring begins	Sept 26, Sat	12:50 PM	Sep 26, Sat	04:50 PM
Release begins	Oct 10, Sat	11:50 AM	Oct 10, Sat	03:50 PM
Bring begins	Oct 26, Mon	12:13 AM	Oct 26, Mon	04:13 AM
Release begins	Nov 9, Mon	02:02 AM	Nov 9, Mon	07:02 AM
Bring begins	Nov 24, Tue	09:55 AM	Nov 24, Tue	02:55 PM
Release begins	Dec 8, Tue	07:52 PM	Dec 9, Wed	12:52 AM
Bring begins	Dec 23, Wed	08:29 PM	Dec 24, Thu	01:29 AM

2027

Lunar Phase   Date & Time —America/New York
        UTC Date & Time

Release begins	Jan 7, Thu	03:25 PM	Jan 7, Thu	08:25 PM
Bring begins	Jan 22, Fri	07:18 AM	Jan 22, Fri	12:18 PM
Release begins	Feb 6, Sat	10:57 AM	Feb 6, Sat	03:57 PM
Bring begins	Feb 20, Sat	06:24 PM	Feb 20, Sat	11:24 PM
Release begins	Mar 8, Mon	04:31 AM	Mar 8, Mon	09:31 AM
Bring begins	Mar 22, Mon	06:44 AM	Mar 22, Mon	10:44 AM
Release begins	Apr 6, Tue	07:53 PM	Apr 6, Tue	11:53 PM
Bring begins	Apr 20, Tue	06:27 PM	Apr 20, Tue	10:27 PM
Release begins	May 6, Thu	07:00 AM	May 6, Thu	11:00 AM
Bring begins	May 20, Thu	06:59 AM	May 20, Thu	10:59 AM
Release begins	Jun 4, Fri	03:41 PM	Jun 4, Fri	07:41 PM
Bring begins	Jun 18, Fri	08:45 PM	Jun 19, Sat	12:45 AM
Release begins	Jul 3, Sat	11:03 PM	Jul 4, Sun	03:03 AM
Bring begins	Jul 18, Sun	11:46 AM	Jul 18, Sun	03:46 PM
Release begins	Aug 2, Mon	06:06 AM	Aug 2, Mon	10:06 AM
Bring begins	Aug 17, Tue	03:30 AM	Aug 17, Tue	07:30 AM
Release begins	Aug 31, Tue	01:42 PM	Aug 31, Tue	05:42 PM
Bring begins	Sep 15, Wed	07:05 PM	Sept 15, Wed	11:05 PM
Release begins	Sep 29, Wed	10:36 PM	Sept 30, Thu	02:36 AM
Bring begins	Oct 15, Fri	09:48 AM	Oct 15, Fri	01:48 PM
Release begins	Oct 29, Fri	09:36 AM	Oct 29, Fri	01:36 PM

Bring begins	Nov 13, Sat	10:27 PM	Nov 14, Sun	03:27 AM
Release begins	Nov 27, Sat	10:25 PM	Nov 28, Sun	03:25 AM
Bring begins	Dec 13, Mon	11:10 AM	Dec 13, Mon	04:10 PM
Release begins	Dec 27, Mon	03:13 PM	Dec 27, Mon	08:13 PM

2028

Lunar Phase   Date & Time America/New York
                    UTC Date & Time

Bring begins	Jan 11, Tue	11:04 PM	Jan 12, Wed	04:04 AM
Release begins	Jan 26, Wed	10:14 AM	Jan 26, Wed	03:14 PM
Bring begins	Feb 10, Thu	10:04 AM	Feb 10, Thu	03:04 PM
Release begins	Feb 25, Fri	05:38 AM	Feb 25, Fri	10:38 AM
Bring begins	Mar 10, Fri	08:06 PM	Mar 11, Sat	01:06 AM
Release begins	Mar 26, Sun	12:33 AM	Mar 26, Sun	04:33 AM
Bring begins	Apr 9, Sun	06:26 AM	Apr 9, Sun	10:26 AM
Release begins	Apr 24, Mon	03:49 PM	Apr 24, Mon	07:49 PM
Bring begins	May 8, Mon	03:49 PM	May 8, Mon	07:49 PM
Release begins	May 24, Wed	04:17 AM	May 24, Wed	08:17 AM
Bring begins	Jun 7, Wed	02:09 AM	Jun 7, Wed	06:09 AM
Release begins	Jun 22, Thu	02:28 PM	Jun 22, Thu	06:28 PM
Bring begins	Jul 6, Thu	02:12 PM	Jul 6, Thu	06:12 PM

Release begins	Jul 21, Fri	11:02 PM	Jul 22, Sat	03:02 AM
Bring begins	Aug 5, Sat	04:11 AM	Aug 5, Sat	08:11 AM
Release begins	Aug 20, Sun	06:44 AM	Aug 20, Sun	10:44 AM
Bring begins	Sep 3, Sun	07:49 PM	Sept 3, Sun	11:49 PM
Release begins	Sep 18, Mon	02:24 PM	Sept 18, Mon	06:24 PM
Bring begins	Oct 3, Tue	12:26 PM	Oct 3, Tue	04:26 PM
Release begins	Oct 17, Tue	10:57 PM	Oct 18, Wed	02:57 AM
Bring begins	Nov 2, Thu	05:19 AM	Nov 2, Thu	09:19 AM
Release begins	Nov 16, Thu	08:18 AM	Nov 16, Thu	01:18 PM
Bring begins	Dec 1, Fri	08:41 PM	Dec 2, Sat	01:41 AM
Release begins	Dec 15, Fri	09:07 PM	Dec 16, Sat	02:07 AM
Bring begins	Dec 31, Sun	11:49 AM	Dec 31, Sun	04:49 PM

2029

Lunar Phase	Date & Time America/New York		UTC Date & Time	
Release begins	Jan 14, Sun	12:26 PM	Jan 14, Sun	05:26 PM
Bring begins	Jan 30, Tue	01:04 AM	Jan 30, Tue	06:04 AM
Release begins	Feb 13, Tue	05:33 AM	Feb 13, Tue	10:33 AM
Bring begins	Feb 28, Wed	12:11 PM	Febr 28, Wed	05:11 PM
Release begins	Mar 15, Thu	12:21 AM	Mar 15, Thu	04:21 AM
Bring begins	Mar 29, Thu	10:27 PM	Mar 30, Fri	02:27 AM

Release begins	Apr 13, Fri	05:42 PM	Apr 13, Fri	09:42 PM
Bring begins	Apr 28, Sat	06:37 AM	Apr 28, Sat	10:37 AM
Release begins	May 13, Sun	09:43 AM	May 13, Sun	01:43 PM
Bring begins	May 27, Sun	02:38 PM	May 27, Sun	06:38 PM
Release begins	Jun 11, Mon	11:51 PM	Jun 12, Tue	03:51 AM
Bring begins	Jun 25, Mon	11:23 PM	Jun 26, Tue	03:23 AM
Release begins	Jul 11, Wed	11:52 AM	Jul 11, Wed	03:52 PM
Bring begins	Jul 25, Wed	09:36 AM	Jul 25, Wed	01:36 PM
Release begins	Aug 9, Thu	09:56 PM	Aug 10, Fri	01:56 AM
Bring begins	Aug 23, Thu	09:52 PM	Aug 24, Fri	01:52 AM
Release begins	Sept 8, Sat	06:45 AM	Sept 8, Sat	10:45 AM
Bring begins	Sept 22, Sat	12:30 PM	Sept 22, Sat	04:30 PM
Release begins	Oct 7, Sun	03:15 PM	Oct 7, Sun	07:15 PM
Bring begins	Oct 22, Mon	05:29 AM	Oct 22, Mon	09:29 AM
Release begins	Nov 5, Mon	11:24 PM	Nov 6, Tue	04:24 AM
Bring begins	Nov 20, Tue	11:04 PM	Nov 21, Wed	04:04 AM
Release begins	Dec 5, Wed	09:53 AM	Dec 5, Wed	02:53 PM
Bring begins	Dec 20, Thu	05:47 PM	Dec 20, Thu	10:47 PM

2030

Lunar Phase	Date & Time America/New York UTC Date & Time			
Release begins	Jan 3, Thu	09:51 PM	Jan 4, Fri	02:51 AM
Bring begins	Jan 19, Sat	10:56 AM	Jan 19, Sat	03:56 PM
Release begins	Feb 2, Sat	11:09 AM	Feb 2, Sat	04:09 PM
Bring begins	Feb 18, Mon	01:22 AM	Feb 18, Mon	06:22 AM
Release begins	Mar 4, Mon	01:37 AM	Mar 4, Mon	06:37 AM
Bring begins	Mar 19, Tue	01:58 PM	Mar 19, Tue	05:58 PM
Release begins	Apr 2, Tue	06:04 PM	Apr 2, Tue	10:04 PM
Bring begins	Apr 17, Wed	11:21 PM	Apr 18, Thu	03:21 AM
Release begins	May 2, Thu	10:13 AM	May 2, Thu	02:13 PM
Bring begins	May 17, Fri	07:20 AM	May 17, Fri	11:20 AM
Release begins	Jun 1, Sat	02:22 AM	Jun 1, Sat	06:22 AM
Bring begins	Jun 15, Sat	02:41 PM	Jun 15, Sat	06:41 PM
Release begins	Jun 30, Sun	05:35 PM	Jun 30, Sun	09:35 PM
Bring begins	Jul 14, Sun	10:11 PM	Jul 15, Mon	02:11 AM
Release begins	Jul 30, Tue	07:11 AM	Jul 30, Tue	11:11 AM
Bring begins	Aug 13, Tue	06:44 AM	Aug 13, Tue	10:44 AM
Release begins	Aug 28, Wed	07:07 PM	Aug 28, Wed	11:07 PM
Bring begins	Sep 11, Wed	05:17 PM	Sept 11, Wed	09:17 PM
Release begins	Sep 27, Fri	05:54 AM	Sept 27, Fri	09:54 AM
Bring begins	Oct 11, Fri	06:46 AM	Oct 11, Fri	10:46 AM

Release begins	Oct 26, Sat	04:17 PM	Oct 26, Sat	08:17 PM
Bring begins	Nov 9, Sat	10:31 PM	Nov 10, Sun	03:31 AM
Release begins	Nov 25, Mon	01:47 AM	Nov 25, Mon	06:47 AM
Bring begins	Dec 9, Mon	05:42 PM	Dec 9, Mon	10:42 PM
Release begins	Dec 24, Tue	12:33 PM	Dec 24, Tue	05:33 PM

Colors and Their Meanings

Here are the meanings of different candle colors in general:

White candles-Destruction of negative energy, peace, truth and purity

Purple candles- Spiritual awareness, wisdom, tranquility

Lavender Candles– Intuition, Paranormal, Peace, Healing

Blue and Deep Blue Candles– Meditation, Healing, Forgiveness, Inspiration, Fidelity, Happiness, and opening lines of Communication.

Green Candles– Money, Fertility, Luck, Abundance, Health (not to be used when diagnosed with Cancer), Success

Rose and Pink Colored Candles– Positive self-love, friendship, harmony, joy

Yellow Candles- Realizing and manifesting thoughts, opening up communication, confidence, bringing plans into action, creativity, intelligence, mental clarity, clairvoyance.

Orange Candles– Joy, energy, education, strength attraction, stimulation

Red or Deep red Candles– Passion, energy, love, lust, relationships, sex, vitality, courage.

Black Candles– Protection, absorption and destruction of negative energy and also repelling negative energy from others

Silver candle– Goddess or feminine energy, remove negativity, psychic development, money

Gold candle– Male energy, Solar energy, fortune, spiritual

attainment, money.

Candle colors and Days:

Sunday– Gold or yellow candles

Monday– Silver, Grey or White

Tuesday-Red

Wednesday-Purple

Thursday– Blue

Friday-Green

Saturday– Black or Purple

Magik Herbs

This list is in no way complete, but it is a starting spot for your own magik research. Make sure to powder each herb, reducing the dried herb to a coarse powder, using a spice grinder or a coffee mill. Add while making candles, or use with an existing candle after anointing it with a base oil, such as almond oil or mineral oil.

- Lavender: Often used for purification, relaxation, and promoting peaceful environments.
- Rosemary: Associated with memory, protection, and warding off negative energies.
- Sage: Used for cleansing and purifying spaces, objects, or people.

- Mugwort: Thought to enhance psychic abilities and lucid dreaming.
- Chamomile: Associated with tranquility, healing, and attracting positive energy.
- Basil: Used for protection, love, and wealth attraction.
- Mint: Often used for healing and enhancing communication.
- Thyme: Associated with courage, purification, and warding off negativity.
- Rose: Used for love spells and enhancing relationships.
- Cinnamon: Thought to boost energy, aid in manifestation, and bring prosperity.
- Dandelion: Associated with divination and wishing spells.
- Yarrow: Used for psychic abilities, love spells, and protection.
- Bay leaves: Often used for wish magic and manifestation.
- Frankincense: Used for purification, meditation, and spiritual practices.
- Myrrh: Associated with healing, protection, and banishing negativity.
- Patchouli: Often used for attracting love, money, and grounding.
- Jasmine: Associated with attracting love,

sensuality, and enhancing psychic abilities.

- Hibiscus: Used for attracting love, divination, and enhancing beauty.
- Nettle: Thought to remove negativity and create protective barriers.
- Vervain: Often used for protection, purification, and empowerment.

Magik Oils

This is a list of the most common oil used in Magik.

- Frankincense Oil: Often used for protection, purification, and spiritual elevation. It is believed to aid in connecting with higher realms and divine energies.
- Myrrh Oil: Associated with healing, purification, and banishing negative energies. It's commonly used in rituals and spells for protection and transformation.
- Lavender Oil: Known for its calming and soothing properties, lavender oil is often used in spells related to relaxation, love, and peacefulness.
- Rose Oil: Symbolizing love and beauty, rose oil is used in rituals for romance, self-love, and matters of the heart.

- Sandalwood Oil: Used for spiritual awareness, meditation, and grounding. It's believed to promote a sense of inner peace and balance.
- Cinnamon Oil: Associated with prosperity, success, and protection. Cinnamon oil is often used to attract wealth and positive energy.
- Patchouli Oil: Often linked to fertility, passion, and attracting love. It's also used in money and prosperity spells.
- Peppermint Oil: Known for its invigorating and stimulating properties, peppermint oil is used for energy, purification, and mental clarity.
- Cedarwood Oil: Used for protection, purification, and grounding. It's associated with strength and stability.
- Eucalyptus Oil: Believed to have healing and cleansing properties. It's often used for purification and to clear away negative energies.
- Bergamot Oil: Associated with happiness, joy, and success. Bergamot oil is used to bring positive energy and attract good fortune.
- Jasmine Oil: Symbolizing mysticism and sensuality, jasmine oil is used in spells related to love, attraction, and spiritual growth.
- Lemon Oil: Used for purification, cleansing, and promoting mental clarity. Lemon oil is believed to remove obstacles and negative influences.

- Orange Oil: Known for its uplifting and positive energy, orange oil is used in spells for happiness, creativity, and success.
- Mugwort Oil: Associated with divination, psychic abilities, and protection during astral travel and dreamwork.

ABOUT THE AUTHOR

Dave is an author of adult fantasy (The Furies series) as well as author of occult books about magick.

David began working ritual magick back in the 1970s. He took a brief break, then used the power of this magick to create a photography career which took him to Los Angeles and work as a photographer for multiple magazines.

David has studied magick in all forms, and in 2018, released a three-part magick instruction course in High Magick. Thousands of students have benefited from David's unique teaching style, making ceremonial magick accessible to everyone.

This book on Candle Magik is the first book in his Magik for Everyone Series.

Dave also has a series on High Magik where he explores the magik of classic gods and daemons, and a series on Grecian Magick, exploring the aspects of ceremonial magick with the gods and goddesses of ancient Greece.

Dave's Facebook Page:

https://www.facebook.com/DavePsychic/

Secrets of Magick Facebook Group:

https://www.facebook.com/groups/secretsofmagick

Join the Grecian Magick Facebook group!

https://www.facebook.com/groups/grecianmagick

Dave's webpage, book readings and his services:

https://davepsychic.com

Then his e-learning website for magik classes

https://highmagikacademy.com

Sigils for this book are housed at

https://davepsychic.com/goddesses-of-hm-sigils/

Magick Books by David Thompson

Available as EPUB, Paperback and Hardcover (*)

Magik For Everyone

- Candle Magik for Everyone

High Magick Series

- High Magick 101
- Daemons of High Magick
- Daemons and the Law of Attraction*
- Magick of Astaroth*
- Daemons of Fortune*

- Lilith, Goddess of Darkness and Light*
- Asmodeus King of Daemons*
- Goddesses of High Magik

Grecian Magick Series
- Magick of Apollo
- Magick of Hermes
- Magick of Aphrodite
- Magick of Fortuna*
- Greco-Roman Wealth Magick*
- Magick of the Sirens/Magick of the Muses

Fiction Novels by David Thompson

The Furies Series
- ☐ Angels of Vengeance
- ☐ Descent into Tartarus
- ☐ Furies: Beginnings
- ☐ Brianna: Making of a Fury